# Union Growth and the Business Cycle

# Warwick Studies in Industrial Relations

General Editors: G. S. Bain and H. A. Clegg

**Also in this series**

*Trade Unions under Collective Bargaining*
Hugh Clegg
*Social Values and Industrial Relations*
Richard Hyman and Ian Brough
*British Employment Statistics*
D. I. MacKay and N. K. Buxton
*Industrial Relations in Fleet Street*
Keith Sisson
*Industrial Relations and the*
*Limits of Law*
Brian Weekes, Michael Mellish,
Linda Dickens, John Lloyd
*Social Stratification and Trade Unionism\**
G. S. Bain, David Coates, Valerie Ellis
*Workplace and Union\**
Ian Boraston, Hugh Clegg, Malcolm Rimmer
*Piecework Bargaining\**
William Brown
*Disputes Procedure in Action\**
Richard Hyman
*The Docks after Devlin\**
Michael Mellish
*Race and Industrial Conflict\**
Malcolm Rimmer

*PUBLISHED BY HEINEMANN EDUCATIONAL BOOKS

# Union Growth and the Business Cycle

AN ECONOMETRIC ANALYSIS

## George Sayers Bain

*Director,*
*SSRC Industrial Relations Research Unit,*
*University of Warwick*

## Farouk Elsheikh

*Lecturer in Econometrics,*
*University of Warwick, and*
*Associate Fellow,*
*SSRC Industrial Relations Research Unit*

BASIL BLACKWELL·OXFORD

*British Library Cataloguing in Publication Data*

Bain, George Sayers
    Union growth and the business cycle : an
    econometric analysis. — (Warwick studies
    in industrial relations).
    Index.
    ISBN 0-631-16650-5
    1. Title  2. Elsheikh, Farouk  3. Series
    331.88  HD 6490.G/
    Business cycles.
    Trade unions.

Typeset in IBM Press Roman by
Preface Ltd., Salisbury, Wilts.
and printed in Great Britain by
Billing and Sons Ltd., Guildford and London

# Contents

## Contents

# List of Figures

# List of Tables

## List of Tables

In Memory of

JOHN RICHARD CLARKE
1944–1973

*A Friend and Colleague*

# Editors' Foreword

Warwick University's first undergraduates were admitted in 1965. The teaching of industrial relations began a year later, and in 1967 a one-year graduate course leading to an MA in Industrial Relations was introduced. Research in industrial relations also commenced in 1967 with a grant from the Clarkson Trustees, and in 1970 received a major impetus when the Social Science Research Council established its Industrial Relations Research Unit at Warwick.

The series of Warwick Studies in Industrial Relations was launched in 1972 as the main vehicle for the publication of the results of Unit projects. It is also intended to include research carried out by staff teaching industrial relations in the University, and, where it merits publication, the work of graduate students.

The present monograph, written by the Director of the Unit and a colleague in the Department of Economics, is concerned with national patterns of union growth in several Western countries. These patterns are characterized by cyclical fluctuations of varying amplitude and duration, and this study attempts to assess the extent to which they can be related to the business cycle and, in particular, to such individual components of the cycle as the cost of living, unemployment, and wages. The monograph is part of a wider project, begun under the direction of the late Allan Flanders, which is concerned with developing and validating a general theory of the determinants of union growth. A future volume will deal with determinants other than the business cycle and with patterns of union growth in particular industries, occupations, and geographical regions.

George Bain
Hugh Clegg

# Acknowledgments

This study rests upon a large volume of statistical data and analysis, and we are indebted to Margaret Morgan for so efficiently and patiently processing the data, steering them through the computer, and tabulating the results; to Annemarie Flanders, Anne Heape, and Muriel Stanley for typing successive drafts of a difficult manuscript so quickly and accurately; to Jennifer Kavanagh for removing numerous stylistic infelicities; and to Judith Carver for compiling the index.

We wish to thank Ian G. Sharpe of the University of Sydney as well as Orley Ashenfelter of Princeton University and John Pencavel of Stanford University for making available to us the data which they used to test their models of union growth. We are also grateful to John Pencavel for reading our manuscript and for making several suggestions which strengthened our argument.

Several other academic colleagues also read all or part of the manuscript and gave us the benefit of their comments and criticism. They include Philip Bentley of Flinders University, David Brody of the University of California, Walter Galenson of Cornell University, Ross Martin of La Trobe University, Bob Sleeper of the City University of New York, and George Zis of the University of Manchester. Our colleagues at Warwick also gave us the benefit of their advice, and we are particularly grateful to William Brown, Hugh Clegg, David Deaton, Joe England, Robert Lindley, Bob Price, Graham Pyatt, Keith Sisson, Paul Stoneman, and Barry Thomas. In expressing our gratitude to all these people, we stress that they do not necessarily share any of the opinions we express. For these and any shortcomings which remain in spite of their efforts, we alone are responsible.

Finally, we would like to thank Carol and Nahed for their encouragement and patience while the study was being undertaken, and for enduring our absences in Kuwait and England while we collaborated on the final draft of the manuscript.

George Bain
Farouk Elsheikh

# 1
# Introduction

This monograph is part of a projected series of volumes on the subject of union growth. Its objective is to develop and verify a theory of fairly general applicability in the sense that it helps to account for union growth in different countries; in different industries, occupations, and regions within these countries; and in different historical periods.

The first volume in the series will be published shortly.[1] It deals with various theoretical, conceptual, and methodological questions which arise in studying union growth. It also provides data on the aggregate patterns of union growth in Australia, Canada, Denmark, Germany, Norway, Sweden, the United Kingdom, and the United States, and, where possible, on the industrial, occupational, and regional patterns of union growth within these countries.[2]

The present volume is the second in the series. It is concerned entirely with national aggregate patterns of union growth. Some of the data which the first volume presents on these patterns are summarized in Figure 1.1. It shows the annual rate of change in total union membership in Australia, Sweden, the United Kingdom, and the United States over several decades. The period selected for analysis varies from country to country and was determined by data availability. The earliest date in any country is 1893 and the latest is 1970, the last year for which data were available when the study began. Figure 1.1 reveals that the annual rate of change in union membership has fluctuated between −11 and +19 per cent in Australia, between −10 and +25 per cent in Sweden, between −26 and +18 per cent in the United Kingdom, and between −19 and +30 per cent in the United States. In short, the growth of aggregate unionism is characterized by cyclical fluctuations of varying amplitude and duration.

Explaining these cyclical fluctuations is one of the fundamental

1. G. S. Bain and R. J. Price, *Profiles of Union Growth: A Comparative Statistical Portrait of Eight Countries* (Oxford: Blackwell, forthcoming).
2. See *ibid.* for the reasons these eight countries have been chosen for analysis.

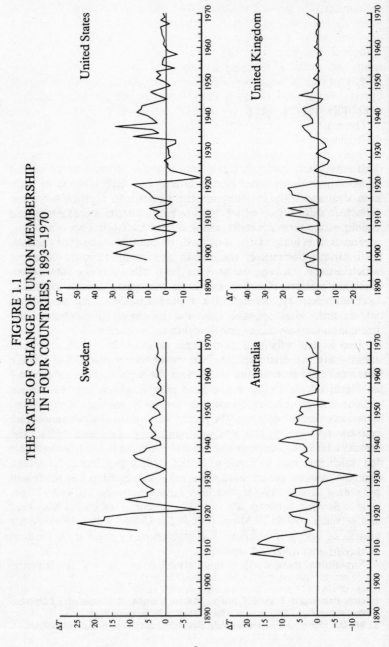

FIGURE 1.1
THE RATES OF CHANGE OF UNION MEMBERSHIP
IN FOUR COUNTRIES, 1893–1970

tasks which an adequate general theory of union growth must accomplish. The present volume makes a start on this task. It does so primarily by assessing the extent to which the fluctuations in aggregate unionism are related to the business cycle and, in particular, to such individual components of the cycle as the cost of living, unemployment, and wages. The following analysis also takes into account some aspects of the social and political environment within which unions operate. But it does so only in a limited way; a further volume will deal more fully with the social and political determinants of union growth.

The search for an explanation of aggregate union growth begins with the business cycle because it is a quantifiable phenomenon. This is not to imply that the quantifiable is necessarily more important than the qualitative, but to suggest that when some of the factors under consideration readily lend themselves to quantification, as is the case here, then at least in the first instance they should be separated from the others and analysed by means of econometric techniques. For these techniques are generally more effective than the human eye in drawing inferences from a large mass of quantitative data. Moreover, they enable the relative importance of the quantifiable variables to be established fairly precisely. And by so doing, they give a better idea of the weight which any subsequent analysis should assign to the qualitative variables.

Econometric techniques facilitate the analysis of quantitative data, but acquiring and analysing the data are nevertheless difficult and time-consuming tasks. Indeed, the difficulties and amount of work involved explain why four of the eight countries included in the first volume have been omitted from the present monograph. The United States and Canada have very similar industrial relations systems and to have included them both would have greatly increased the work load without significantly advancing the following analysis. The United States was preferred to Canada, partly because the relevant American data are more plentiful and cover a longer period, and partly because Canadian business and union activity is less fundamental in the sense that much of it is transmitted from the United States.[3] A similar argument applies to Denmark, Norway, and Sweden. Sweden was

---

3. See, for example, Irving Brecher and S. S. Reisman, *Canada-United States Economic Relations* (Ottawa: Queen's Printer, Royal Commission on Canada's Economic Prospects, 1957), especially chaps. 2–5 and 12. See also, John Crispo, *International Unionism: A Study in Canadian-American Relations* (Toronto: McGraw-Hill, 1967).

Since the statistical work for this monograph was completed, R. Swidinsky has constructed an econometric model of union growth for Canada. It demonstrates, among other things, that union growth in Canada is closely associated with that in the United States. See 'Trade Union Growth in Canada: 1911–1970', *Relations Industrielles*, XXIX, no. 3 (1974), 435–51.

preferred on the grounds that its data are more plentiful and reliable, especially before the Second World War, than those of Denmark and Norway. Ideally, Germany should have been included, but it has no membership data for the period 1932–46, and its series on such potentially important explanatory variables as the cost of living and wages were so distorted by the hyperinflation of the early 1920s that these years would also have had to be excluded from the analysis.

Although this monograph relies heavily upon econometric techniques, Chapter 2 begins the analysis in a non-technical way by examining the major theories which have been advanced to explain the growth of aggregate unionism. Aspects of these theories have recently been quantified and tested within the framework of econometric models, and these are assessed in Chapter 3. All of these models possess various weaknesses, so Chapter 4 specifies an alternative model of union growth and applies it to data for the United Kingdom. The model is initially developed in relation to the United Kingdom because its data are most familiar and of easiest access to the authors, they cover the longest period, and have previously received relatively little attention. Chapter 5 takes the general form of the model developed for the United Kingdom and estimates it using data for the United States, Australia, and Sweden. The concluding chapter draws the various parts of the analysis together and considers some objections which might be raised against the model.

Parts of Chapters 3, 4, and 5 will be easier to understand if the reader has some familiarity with regression analysis, a technique for investigating the relationship between a dependent variable and a set of explanatory variables.[4] Although widely used by labour economists and many other social scientists, regression analysis is less frequently employed by industrial relations specialists and labour historians. Since the authors wish to communicate with the latter as much as with the former, the more technical aspects of the analysis have been placed in footnotes and appendices. An attempt has also been made to translate the significance of the results into English which is free of statistical jargon. A number of statistical terms have nevertheless had to be used in the main body of the text; these are explained in the appendices which appear at the end of the monograph.

---

4. For an introduction to regression analysis, see W. J. Reichmann, *Use and Abuse of Statistics* (Harmondsworth, Middlesex: Penguin, 1964), chap. 10; and M. J. Moroney, *Facts from Figures* (Harmondsworth, Middlesex: Penguin, 1956), chap. 16. See also M. J. C. Surrey, *An Introduction to Econometrics* (Oxford: Clarendon Press, 1974); and A. Koutsoyiannis, *Theory of Econometrics* (London: Macmillan, 1973), chaps. 4–7.

# 2
# Theories of Union Growth

The question of union growth is not approached with a *tabula rasa*. Virtually every union history says something about the subject, as do a great many other works dealing with trade unions. But most of them have been content merely to describe the contours of union growth and to offer one or two explanatory hints. They have not tried to generalize broadly, and even less to theorize systematically, about the causes of union growth.

But a few writers have. Most of them have been based in the United States and they have been primarily interested in explaining developments in that country. The relevance of their basic arguments is not necessarily restricted to the United States, however, and this chapter examines them to see what general insights they have to offer into the process of union growth. It is concerned not only with more recent writers who have attempted to gather all the causes of union growth into a comprehensive and systematic theory but also with earlier writers who theorized in a more fragmentary and less systematic fashion. In both cases, it focuses upon those theoretical notions which have particular relevance for national aggregate patterns of union growth.

## Early Theorists

The earliest writers on union growth related it primarily to the business cycle. Indeed, Samuel Gompers, the first president of the American Federation of Labor, was so impressed with the way in which unionization had 'grown with each year of industrial activity and receded to some degree with each industrial depression' that he referred to this phenomenon as the 'law of growth in organized labor'.[1] The validity of this 'law' was confirmed by the academics of his day.

Commons and his associates at the University of Wisconsin observed

1. *Report of Proceedings*, 24th Annual Convention of the AFL (1904), 15–17.

5

that 'cycles of prosperity and depression have characterized all lands during the expansion of industry and credit in the nineteenth century', and they argued that 'labour movements in all countries pursue these cycles.' In their view, the explanation of this correlation was that

during a time when the level of prices is rising, employers generally are making profits, are multiplying sales, are enlarging their capital, are running full time and overtime, are calling for more labor, and are able to pay higher wages. On the other hand, the cost of living and the hours of labor are increased, and workmen, first as individuals, then as organizations, are impelled to demand both higher wages and reduced hours. Consequently, after prices are well on the way upward the 'labor movement' emerges in the form of unions and strikes, and these are at first successful. Then the employers begin their counter-organization, and the courts are appealed to. The unions are sooner or later defeated, and when the period of depression ensues, with its widespread unemployment, the labor movement either subsides or changes its form to political or socialistic agitation, to ventures in cooperation or communism, or to other panaceas.

Commons and his colleagues felt that this 'cycle has been so consistently repeated' that they divided American trade union history into distinct periods on the basis of the business cycle as measured by the index of wholesale prices.[2]

The Wisconsin School based their case upon a detailed study of the development of the American labour movement in the nineteenth century. Since this is a period for which there is a dearth of reliable data on aggregate union membership trends, they were unable to present much evidence directly linking the business cycle to union size. In fact, their evidence was concerned more with the character of the labour movement than with its size, and it demonstrated that unions tend to rely upon industrial action in times of prosperity but turn to political action in periods of depression.[3]

2. The quotations in this paragraph are from John R. Commons *et al.*, *History of Labour in the United States*, I (New York: Macmillan, 1918), 10–11; and John R. Commons and Helen L. Sumner, *A Documentary History of American Industrial Society*, V (Cleveland: A. H. Clark, 1911), 19. See also Selig Perlman, *A History of Trade Unionism in the United States* (New York: Macmillan, 1923), 275–7.

3. See Commons *et al.*, *op. cit.*, 11–12 *et passim*. Similar evidence is presented for the United States by Robert F. Hoxie, *Trade Unionism in the United States* (New York: Appleton, 1921), 81–7, and for both the United States and Great Britain by W. B. Catlin, *The Labor Problem in the United States and Great Britain*, revised edition (New York: Harper, 1926), chap. 9. The argument that the business cycle determines not only the size but also the character of the labour movement is beyond the scope of this study and is not considered here.

The Wisconsin School's argument that the size of the labour movement was determined by the business cycle was supported, however, by the more quantitative approach of Weyforth and Barnett of Johns Hopkins University. Weyforth took the annual production of pig iron in the United States as an index of business activity, and found that it was positively related to the growth of union membership in the state of New York between 1894 and 1912. He felt that this positive association was

nothing more than we should expect; for there are several important reasons why trade-union membership is decidedly influenced by the general state of business. In the first place, during a period of depression when there is much unemployment, it becomes difficult or impossible for many members to keep up their dues. Many lapses occur for this reason. Secondly, not only is it harder to hold old members, but it is more difficult to obtain new ones. When many people out of employment are waiting to take the workman's place, he is less inclined to run the risk of losing his job by antagonizing his employer through trade-union activities than at times when jobs are plentiful. Finally, the union occupies a weaker strategical position in times of depression than in times of prosperity. When business is active, employers are, generally speaking, reaping their harvest. Hence an interruption of their business is extremely undesirable, and often they may prefer to yield to the demands of their workmen rather than undergo the losses incident to a shut-down. Moreover, even in case the employer is inclined to fight, he will find it more difficult to recruit his force with competent non-union workmen because there is a smaller labor supply of the unemployed available than in times of depression. But in times of depression not only is the employer, because of the large supply of unemployed workmen, better able to make a fight against the union, but he is also less disinclined to do so, since with business running low, a strike of his men may provide a convenient excuse for shutting down his plant.[4]

Barnett concentrated on assembling a large amount of data on union membership in the United States as a whole for the period 1897–1920. But he noted that 'changes in membership are closely connected with changes in business conditions.'[5]

Barnett's work on union membership statistics was carried on by Wolman. He refined and extended Barnett's figures to 1923 and argued

4. William O. Weyforth, *The Organizability of Labor* (Baltimore: Johns Hopkins Press, 1917), 247–8.
5. George E. Barnett, 'Growth of Labor Organization in the United States, 1897–1914', *Quarterly Journal of Economics*, XXX (August 1916), 786; and 'The Present Position of American Trade Unionism', *American Economic Review Papers and Proceedings*, 24th Annual Meeting (December 1921), 44–55.

that the trends they revealed generally supported the business cycle theory.[6] His interest in union growth continued, and in 1936 he published data on union membership covering the period up to 1934. He was forced to conclude from an analysis of this data that during the prosperity of the 1920s the business cycle theory had 'failed to work'. In fact, he argued that 'the very prosperity of the period and the generally high standards of wages and employment acted, apparently, in most classes of industry to retard rather than to accelerate the pace of union growth.'[7]

Davis made a major contribution to the debate in a paper published in 1941.[8] He claimed that the early business cycle theorists had failed to distinguish sufficiently between rises in prices and improvements in business conditions. He pointed out that business prosperity and rising prices do not necessarily go together, and offered several reasons why the latter was more important than the former in the process of union growth. To begin with, wage rates tend to lag behind marked increases in prices, and his reading of labour history suggested that a fear of a fall in the standard of living was the major grievance motivating employees to join unions. He stressed that unions were primarily 'defensive' organizations which arose not so much to increase workingmen's living standards as to prevent a decline in a standard which they already enjoyed. Secondly, he argued that 'a period of rapidly rising prices is nearly (but not quite) always a period of increasing production and decreasing unemployment, so that the favorable factors of prosperity all apply.' Thirdly, increases in labour costs can more easily be passed along to customers in periods of rapidly rising prices, and he therefore felt that employers would be less hostile about recognizing and negotiating with unions in such periods. Finally, he claimed that union growth correlates more closely with rising prices than with the prosperity phase of the business cycle because price increases affect all workers, while the cycle is primarily restricted to the capital goods industries and leaves workers in most other industries largely unaffected.

He supported this reasoning with a considerable amount of empirical evidence. To begin with, he compared changes in general business conditions[9] with movements in union membership in France, Germany, the United Kingdom, and the United States from the 1890s to the 1930s. He found that in 42 (68 per cent) of the 61 cases of prosperity

6. Leo Wolman, *The Growth of American Trade Unions, 1880–1923* (New York: National Bureau of Economic Research, 1924), 33, 37, and 39.
7. Leo Wolman, *Ebb and Flow in Trade Unionism* (New York: National Bureau of Economic Research, 1936), 162–3.
8. Horace B. Davis, 'The Theory of Union Growth', *Quarterly Journal of Economics*, LV (August 1941), 611–37.
9. Unlike such previous writers as Barnett and Wolman, Davis made clear exactly how he had ascertained the state of business conditions. He dated the various phases of the business cycle by using the pioneering work of W. L. Thorp and

there were marked rises (more than 3 per cent)[10] in union membership, but that in 15 (24 per cent) of such cases union membership declined. Similarly, although 25 (51 per cent) of the 49 cases of business recession and depression were accompanied by falling union membership, there were 14 such cases (28 per cent) in which membership increased sharply.[11] He concluded from these findings that there is an 'inadequate statistical basis' for the 'naive' form of the business cycle theory which holds that 'union growth is positively correlated with prosperity, rising when business is good and falling when business is bad.'

He then compared the movements in union membership with changes in price levels for the same countries and time periods.[12] He found that of the 53 cases in which prices rose markedly (by more than 3 per cent), union membership increased markedly in 41 (77 per cent) and fell in only 8 (15 per cent) of the cases. Similarly, of the 30 cases in which prices fell markedly, union membership decreased in 18 (60 per cent) and increased sharply only in 7 (23 per cent) of the cases. He concluded that 'the evidence seems to indicate that changes in union membership correlate more closely with sharp changes in prices than with "prosperity".'[13]

---

W. C. Mitchell, *Business Annals* (New York: National Bureau of Economic Research, 1926), 75–87. Their work has the advantage of using a uniform method for all the four countries with which Davis was concerned.

10. Since the secular trend of union membership was upward in all four countries during the period covered, Davis considered a rise of less than 3 per cent to be insignificant.

11. A similar but less rigorous analysis of the relationship between movements in union membership and changes in business conditions was undertaken for the United Kingdom by N. Barou, *British Trade Unions* (London: Gollancz, 1947), 86–7, 245–6.

12. Davis was inconsistent in the way he measured prices. Although a cost-of-living or retail price index is available for all four countries, he used such an index only for the United States. For the remaining countries, he used the index of wholesale prices.

13. While his conclusion is true, it is somewhat overstated. In trying to show that union membership correlates more closely with prices than with the general state of business conditions, Davis grouped the 'recession' and 'depression' phases of the business cycle together but treated the 'revival' and 'prosperity' phases separately. Indeed, he treated the evidence for the revival phase as being irrelevant to the testing of the prosperity thesis. Why he did this is not altogether clear. Just as Davis seems to have assumed that the early business cycle theorists were using the term 'depression' broadly to include 'recession', it is not inconsistent with their argument to suggest that they were using the term 'prosperity' in a similar fashion to include 'revival'. In any case, if the evidence for prosperity and revival is grouped together, then union membership increases markedly in 72 per cent and falls in only 21 per cent of the cases. The price variable still performs better than the general state of business conditions, but not by such a wide margin. See Davis, *op. cit.*, 615, table 1.

Davis presented a most impressive case. But in claiming that the early business cycle theorists did not distinguish sufficiently between price increases and prosperity, he was being unfair to at least the Wisconsin School which, as the above quotation from their work makes clear, strongly emphasized the impact of rising prices on living standards as a reason for workers joining unions. While it is true that Commons and his associates suggested that the effect of price increases on union growth arose in part because they are a proxy for the general prosperity of industry, so did Davis. One of the explanations he gave for the increase of union membership during periods of rapidly rising prices was that such periods are generally characterized by the 'favorable factors of prosperity' — increasing production and decreasing unemployment — which increase labour's power. In fact, he cited cases where although prices had risen, production and employment had fallen, with the result that union membership had declined.

Davis emphasized even more strongly that employee grievances generated by rapidly rising prices or any other cause are only a favourable and not a sufficient condition for union growth, for he claimed that

when labor has major new grievances and an improving position in the labor market, unions tend to grow. When labor has no major new grievances or when its position in the labor market is not improving, conditions for organization are not especially favorable; and when labor is economically weak or losing ground in the labor market, though grievances exist and give rise to organization movements, these movements are not likely to result in a general increase in union membership which tends to decline.

He felt that 'the period of the business cycle when labor is most apt to have grievances and to be gaining in economic power is the period of revival from depression' for 'revival is likely to be accompanied by rising prices and increasing employment, while labor has major grievances that have accumulated during the depression.' He examined 20 cases of revival from depression and found that in 16 (80 per cent) of them union membership increased markedly while in only 2 (10 per cent) of them did it decline. He took these findings as providing at least partial support for his view that labour's economic power is as important as its grievances in promoting union growth.[14]

14. The quotations in this paragraph are from *ibid.*, 619–20. It is surprising that Davis should have used such an indirect method to try to prove his case. He felt that the best index of labour's economic power is the state of employment, but claimed that 'employment indexes are still so limited in scope' that they would not permit a conclusive test of the theory. It is not clear what he meant by this remark. But fairly reliable data on unemployment exist for all four countries, and they would probably have permitted a more conclusive test of his argument than the indirect procedure which he adopted.

Davis did not demonstrate, as he implied, that his 'prices theory' was superior to the Wisconsin School's 'prosperity theory'. For they are not two different theories. Rather, as the above discussion makes clear, they employ virtually identical arguments and are, in effect, the same theory. What Davis did demonstrate, and in a more rigorous fashion than ever before, is the empirical strength of the theory that fluctuations in union growth are at least partly determined by fluctuations in economic conditions. In addition, he showed that a price index provides a better specification of this theory than does an index based on a fairly subjective judgment as to the particular point at which one phase of the business cycle gives way to another; at least he demonstrated that the former index is more closely correlated with union membership than the latter. Finally, by revealing that 'revival' is a more favourable time for union growth than 'prosperity', he indicated that 'the direction of the movement of the indexes is more important than their absolute level', a point which has figured prominently in recent research.

## Later Theorists

Although the early writers on union growth generally stressed the significance of the business cycle, most of them were prepared to admit that other factors were also important at least in certain historical contexts. Indeed, Weyforth wrote a lengthy treatise which demonstrated that union growth 'is affected by a great complexity of factors', including the state of public opinion, the degree of urbanization, the management of the union itself, the characteristics of particular groups of workers, the nature of business organization and the attitude of employers, the technical nature of various trades and industries, and the general economic life of the country.[15] Barnett pointed out that the bulk of the total increase in union membership from 1915 to 1920 occurred in the *'war industries par excellence'* — building, metals, clothing, and transportation — and was brought about by the 'intervention of the government in one way or another to preserve industrial peace'.[16] In trying to predict the growth of unionism after 1936, Wolman suggested that in addition to the general state of business conditions, governmental labour and economic policy, the attitude of employers, the state of mind of employees, and the internal relations of the labour movement all had to be taken into account.[17] Davis too stressed that 'a mere analysis of economic conditions does not suffice

15. *op. cit.*
16. 'The Present Position of American Trade Unionism', *op. cit.*, 48.
17. *Ebb and Flow in Trade Unionism, op. cit.*, 148–9.

for an adequate understanding of the ups-and-downs of unionism,' and rounded off his economic analysis by discussing the impact of union leadership, industrialization and technology, and government policies upon union growth.[18]

While acknowledging the importance of these non-economic factors, however, none of the early writers really presented an integrated, systematic multi-causal theory of union growth. Dunlop made the first attempt to do this in 1949.[19] He began by suggesting that it is helpful to distinguish between long-term trends in union growth and short-term variations around these trends. He dealt first with the long-term development of the labour movement. He suggested that two factors are necessary before labour organization will begin to emerge among a group of employees: at least some of them must occupy 'a strategic position in the technological or market structures' so that they can disrupt the process of production and distribution, and most of them must view their opportunities for upward social mobility as being limited and 'look forward to spending a substantial proportion of their lifetime as workmen' in 'the same or similar work community'.[20] Given that labour organization emerges, he argued that there are two additional factors which are decisive in determining the long-term trend of development: such wider community institutions as the courts and governmental administrative agencies, and 'the system of values, the ethos, and the beliefs of the community'.

In trying to account for the short-term deviations from the long-term trend, Dunlop identified seven periods in which the American labour movement had expanded rapidly. He divided these periods into two distinct types: years of war and years of fundamental unrest.[21] He accounted for the rapid rise in union membership during war years almost entirely by developments in the labour market: the sharp rise in the cost of living and the shortage of labour supply relative to demand. Workers joined unions in such periods 'to increase their wages to an extent more closely approximating the rise in prices', and the 'tightness

---

18. *op. cit.*, 625–33.
19. John T. Dunlop, 'The Development of Labor Organization: A Theoretical Framework', *Insights into Labor Issues*, ed. Richard A. Lester and Joseph Shister (New York: Macmillan, 1949), 163–93.
20. Social or occupational immobility may be a favourable condition for union growth but it is not, as Dunlop suggested, a necessary condition. For there is evidence from several countries that workers who expect to rise, or indeed have already risen, out of the 'working class' nevertheless join trade unions. See G. S. Bain, David Coates, and Valerie Ellis, *Social Stratification and Trade Unionism* (London: Heinemann, 1973), 30–33, and 41–4.
21. Dunlop identified the years of war as 1863–72, 1896–1904, 1917–20, and 1941–5, and the years of fundamental unrest as 1827–36, 1881–6, and 1933–7.

in the labor market and the general level of profits enabled the union to achieve results'. In short, he regarded union growth during war years 'as predominantly a market reflex'.

The rapid expansion in union membership during the periods of fundamental unrest resulted, in Dunlop's view, from 'a basic dissatisfaction with the performance of the economic system and the society in general'. He claimed that modern capitalism has moved in long waves or Kondratieff cycles of approximately fifty years in length, with twenty-five years of good times and twenty-five years of bad times, which are to be distinguished from the shorter business cycles.[22] He noted that each of the periods of fundamental unrest came at the bottom of a Kondratieff cycle during which the shorter business cycles had been severe and intense. He concluded that 'after prolonged periods of high unemployment for a substantial number in the work force and after years of downward pressure on wages exerted by price declines,' labour organizations begin to grow and 'are apt to be particularly critical of the fundamental tenets of the society and the economy'.

Writing a few years after Dunlop, Bernstein offered a similar but distinctive analysis of union growth.[23] He began by attacking the business cycle theory. He compared union membership with the business cycle as a whole as measured by the National Bureau of Economic Research's reference cycles,[24] as well as with such key components of the cycle as the cost of living, employment, wholesale prices, and industrial production. He found that the correlation between the National Bureau's cycles and union membership 'is, at best, remote', and that none of the simple correlation coefficients generated by relating union membership to the individual components of the cycle was statistically significant. But he did not completely dismiss the business cycle as a factor in union growth. For although he concluded that 'so capricious a force' is 'useless' for explaining

22. He used the dating scheme offered by Alvin H. Hansen, *Fiscal Policy and Business Cycles* (New York: Norton, 1940), 30; and classified the 'good times' as 1787–1815, 1843–73, 1897–1920, and 1940–, and the 'bad times' as 1815–43, 1873–97, and 1920–40.
23. Irving Bernstein, 'The Growth of American Unions', *American Economic Review*, XLIV (June 1954), 301–18; and 'The Growth of American Unions, 1945–1960', *Labor History*, II (Spring 1961), 131–57. In 'Union Growth and Structural Cycles', *Proceedings of the Industrial Relations Research Association*, VII (December 1954), 202–30, Bernstein advanced a similar analysis but also argued that the rate of union growth was a major determinant of the form of union structure. This argument is not considered here. Unless otherwise indicated, all quotations from Bernstein's work are from the first-mentioned paper.
24. See A. F. Burns and W. C. Mitchell, *Measuring Business Cycles* (New York: National Bureau of Economic Research, 1946).

13

long-term trends, he admitted that it was helpful in accounting for short-term changes in union membership 'in specific historical contexts'.

In analysing short-term growth, he followed Dunlop and divided the periods into those associated with wars and those related to fundamental social unrest. He agreed with Dunlop that business cycle factors, particularly the cost of living, are important in explaining wartime union growth. But, unlike Dunlop, he also stressed the importance of non-economic factors. He felt that 'the social tensions and dislocations that accompany a major war give workers the need to express their discontent' and that 'unionism supplies a vehicle for this purpose.' In addition, he argued that the need of the government to obtain the co-operation of the unions in prosecuting the war enhances their political power, raises their prestige and acceptability, and makes it easier for them to obtain recognition and negotiating rights. This is true not only in critical war industries which the government directly controls but also in privately controlled industries where employers are under government pressure to concede recognition rather than force a strike. Employer hostility to unions is also lessened in war-time as a result of the general shortage of labour and the greater ability to pass on higher wages in rising prices.

A period of social unrest emerges, according to Bernstein, 'only in the wake of a depression so severe as to call into question the very foundations of society'. He noted that in such periods union membership begins to expand not at the depth of the depression but after the upswing has commenced, thereby indicating that 'the cycle exerts a trigger effect under these special circumstances.' The forces that promote union growth in such periods are, in his view, 'of quite different character' to those operating during war-time. The first factor is labour unrest. 'A severe and prolonged depression imposes heavy burdens upon workers and their families, causing them to develop sharp grievances against the existing social order' and to join unions as a form of protest. In addition, a severe depression reveals the ineffectiveness of the economic system and discredits its leading protagonist, the businessman, with the result that 'his voice, no matter how shrill, is not likely to be heard.' These two factors combine to permit the third: intervention by the government to protect the right of workers to organize and to bargain collectively.

In the short run, in Bernstein's view, unions have been 'the beneficiaries of disaster'.[25] In the long run, however, he suggested that

---

25. In addition to wars and severe depressions, Bernstein also mentioned the quality of union leadership as a short-term factor in union growth. He felt it was of little importance in the long run, however, and did not consider it at any length in his analysis.

several 'secular forces' have been at work to increase the size of the American labour movement: the expansion of the labour force which 'has afforded unionism a steadily rising organizable potential', the increasing social acceptability of trade unionism among workers and the community at large, the growing homogeneity of the labour force, and the increasing number of union security provisions in collective agreements.

The arguments advanced by Dunlop and, in particular, by Bernstein have been subjected to considerable criticism.[26] To begin with, Bernstein's data are inadequate in several respects. He neglected to deduct the Canadian members of American unions from his membership series for the United States, and Troy has shown that the failure to do this 'contributes to important differences in results'. Troy has also demonstrated that Bernstein's extrapolated figures for the post-1948 period are generally 'too high' and 'changes are sometimes in the wrong direction or of too small amplitude.'[27] His criticisms are borne out by the more accurate data of both the Bureau of Labor Statistics and the National Bureau of Economic Research which have become available since Bernstein's work was published.[28] Finally, in calculating 'real membership' or the proportion of the labour force organized, Bernstein failed to deduct the non-organizable groups — farmers, proprietors, managers, and officials — from the total civilian labour force. His justification that 'no annual series of the union potential exists' is weak;[29] for such a series could be derived from existing labour force

26. See, in particular, the comments by Charles W. Fristoe, and Harold W. Davey, Edgar M. Jacobs, and John Monroe as well as Bernstein's reply in the *American Economic Review*, XLV (June 1955), 386–93; the comments by Daniel Bell, Lloyd Ulman, and Russell Allen in the *Proceedings of the Industrial Relations Research Association*, VII (December 1954), 231–46; the comments by John T. Dunlop, Eli Ginzberg, Frederick Meyers, Julius Rezler, and Leo Troy in *Labor History*, II (Fall 1961), 361–80; Julius Rezler, *Union Growth Reconsidered: A Critical Analysis of Recent Growth Theories* (New York: Kossuth Foundation, 1961); and Albert A. Blum, 'Why Unions Grow', *Labor History*, IX (Winter 1968), 39–72.

Bernstein used his theory to rebut the claim of Daniel Bell, 'The Next American Labor Movement', *Fortune*, XLVII (April 1953), 120–23 and 201–6, that the American labour movement had reached a saturation level and was unlikely to grow significantly in the future. The future growth or decline of American unionism is beyond the scope of this study, and this aspect of the debate is not considered here.

27. See his comment in *Labor History, op. cit.*, 376–8. See also Bell's comment in *Proceedings of the Industrial Relations Research Association, op. cit.*, 232–3.

28. These are cited in G. S. Bain and R. J. Price, *Profiles of Union Growth* (Oxford: Blackwell, forthcoming).

29. 'The Growth of American Unions, 1945–1960', *op. cit.*, 134.

data, as Rezler has pointed out, 'with less extrapolation than Bernstein uses in computing his union membership series'.[30]

Criticism has also been directed at the way in which Bernstein manipulated and interpreted his data. He could not find a consistent relationship between changes in union membership and the 'major' swings in business activity isolated by the National Bureau of Economic Research. But Ulman has pointed out that 'if one observes movements in the rate, as well as in the direction of change, variations in union membership do conform to (at least) major fluctuations in business activity.' For example, although membership increased during the downswings of 1907–8 and 1937–8 as Bernstein noted, it did so at an appreciably slower rate than in the upswings preceding these two periods. And although membership declined during the upswing of 1921–9, it did so at a slower rate than during the preceding downswing of 1920–21 and the following downswing of 1929–32.[31] Similarly, when Bernstein used a simple regression technique to examine the *individual* relationship between union membership during a given period and the cost of living, employment, wholesale prices, and industrial production in the *same* period, he did not obtain statistically significant results. But Davey, Jacobs, and Monroe have demonstrated that when a multiple regression technique is used to examine the *joint* relationship between union membership during a given period and these four components of the business cycle during the *previous* period, the results produced are significant.[32]

Bernstein's case against the business cycle theory is weakened not only because his statistical assessment of it is insufficiently exhaustive and rigorous but also because his attitude towards it is inconsistent. In

---

30. See his comment in *Labor History, op. cit.*, 370–71.
31. See his comment in the *Proceedings of the Industrial Relations Research Association, op. cit.*, 237–41.
32. They specified a lagged relationship 'because on the downturn union members rarely fall away at once and on the upturn it takes time to launch organization drives to attract new members and regain former members'. See their comment in the *American Economic Review, op. cit.*, 389–90.

Bernstein was quite rightly not unduly impressed by these results since although the multiple regression coefficient is significant at the 5 per cent level, none of the individual coefficients is significant. But his argument in rebuttal that the secular trend had not been removed from any of the statistical series employed by Davey, Jacobs, and Monroe, and the implication that this somehow lessens the significance of their results, is odd, since he did not remove the secular trends from the series he used in his own analysis. In any case, to the extent that Davey, Jacobs, and Monroe obtained significant results, they have 'explained' a significant proportion of both secular and cyclical components of union growth. See Bernstein's reply in the *American Economic Review, op. cit.*, 393.

1954 he argued that the relationship between membership and employment is 'nonexistent', that output or industrial production exhibited 'the least connection with union membership' of all the factors studied, and that the business cycle theory 'is without general validity'. Yet only seven years later, faced with explaining the failure of the labour movement to grow between 1956 and 1960, he reversed his position and claimed that the fundamental reason 'was the failure of the American economy to grow': 'output did not advance significantly,' 'there was a persistent and large lump of unemployment,' and the 'rate of increase in employment perceptibly slowed down'. He concluded that 'the growth of the labor movement is inextricably linked to the growth of the economy.'[33]

It is conceivable, of course, that the effect of the business cycle is historically contingent: it may have an impact upon union growth in one period but not in another. In fact, this is exactly what Bernstein suggested in 1954 when he argued that the 'cycle exerts a contributory influence in specific historical contexts' such as periods of war and fundamental social unrest. Leaving aside the fact that the period 1956–60 was not characterized by wars or fundamental social unrest, the question remains why the business cycle should have an influence upon union growth only in such periods.

The answer which Bernstein gave to this question is not entirely satisfactory. Part of it is based, at least implicitly, upon Dunlop's analysis. Dunlop argued that the intensity of the cycle was greatest during wars and years of social unrest. Indeed, as has already been shown, he went so far as to claim that modern capitalism is characterized by long Kondratieff cycles of business activity which carry the economy to extreme heights and alternately to extreme depths at intervals of about twenty-five years. But he presented no direct evidence concerning these cycles, and their existence is not as 'well established in the analysis of economic fluctuations' as he thought. After 'weighing all the evidence thus far presented', Gordon has concluded that 'the hypothesis that business activity moves in recurring long cycles of fifty to sixty years still remains unconfirmed.'[34] All that has been firmly established is that there have been long-term secular price movements whose peaks have generally been connected with periods of war and whose troughs have generally

---

33. See 'The Growth of American Unions, 1945–1960', *op. cit.*, 157; 'Don't Count the Unions Out', *Challenge* (November 1961); and 'The Growth of American Unions', *op. cit.*, 310–13.
34. R. A. Gordon, *Business Fluctuations* (New York: Harper, 1952), 207. See also George Garvy, 'Kondratieff's Theory of Long Cycles', *Review of Economic Statistics*, XXV (November 1943), 203–20.

been associated with exceptionally large amounts of unemployment and social unrest.[35]

Given that it is these secular movements in prices to which Dunlop was referring, then he did not add much to the debate. For these are the same secular price movements whose importance as a factor in union growth the Wisconsin School pointed to forty years earlier. In fact, Dunlop did not establish the link between these price movements and union membership with any greater precision than had Commons and his associates. He relied upon their rough estimates of union membership for the first four periods in which the American labour movement expanded rapidly, and provided rough estimates of his own for the last three periods. Moreover, his evidence, like theirs, was as much concerned with the character of the labour movement as with its size.[36] In short, this part of Dunlop's work did little more than restate and update the Wisconsin School's pioneering but imprecise argument that the price level is the 'backbone' of American social and political history.

Bernstein basically accepted Dunlop's argument regarding the intensity of the cycle during periods of war and social unrest and added no new evidence of his own on this point. But he did offer another reason why the business cycle should have a particular impact upon union growth during such periods. He suggested, as the above discussion makes clear, that a variety of non-economic factors are at work which reinforce the influence of the cycle.[37] He claimed that although all these factors are favourable to union growth, those operating during wars are 'of quite different character' to those acting in periods of fundamental social unrest. But a closer examination of these factors suggests that they are not as different as Bernstein imagined. For regardless of their form and whether they occur during periods of war or of social unrest, most of them have fundamentally the same effect: to make it easier for unions to obtain recognition and negotiating rights from employers.

Bernstein's failure to emphasize the common nature of the factors which he quite rightly claimed reinforced the workings of the business cycle during periods of war and of social unrest following a severe depression is indicative of the fundamental weakness of the 'disaster'

35. There is considerable doubt whether these secular price movements should be described as 'cycles'. *'Price trends* we have indeed had,' as Hansen has noted, 'but not necessarily long-run *cumulative movements* which can properly be referred to as "long cycles" or "long waves"' which inevitably repeat themselves. See Alvin H. Hansen, *Business Cycles and National Income* (New York: Norton, 1951), 53–76; and Gordon, *op. cit.*, 187–208.
36. See Dunlop, *op. cit.*, 190–92.
37. See pp. 14–15 above for a discussion of these factors.

approach to union growth which he and Dunlop advanced. By concentrating attention on *ad hoc* 'disasters', it tends to underplay the processes by which union growth takes place and to mask the more fundamental and systematic factors which play a role in these processes. In short, wars and depressions are simply 'blunderbuss' variables which obscure more than they reveal about the dynamics of union growth.

By what 'mystical' process, as Blum has asked,[38] does a severe depression cause workers to develop 'sharp grievances against the existing social order' which result in them joining trade unions? What exactly are these 'sharp grievances'? Do they result, as Dunlop claimed, from 'a basic dissatisfaction with the performance of the economic system and the society in general'? And if workers actually are dissatisfied with the whole 'social order' and the performance of 'society in general', then why do they turn to trade unionism rather than to some more encompassing form of evolutionary or revolutionary political activity? If workers' grievances are more narrowly based, then with exactly what aspects of the 'system' are they dissatisfied? Is it the failure of the economy to maintain high levels of employment and earnings which causes their grievances? If it is, why not explicitly say so, and specify the explanatory variables in a more precise and operational form? Similarly, by what process do 'the social tensions and dis-locations that accompany a major war give workers the need to express their discontent' by joining unions? Is this saying anything more than that wars generally cause the cost of living to rise sharply and this, in turn, encourages workers to unionize in order to maintain their living standards? If it is, then why not spell out the additional factors which create 'discontent' among workers during war-time? If it is not, then why mystify the operation of the business cycle by using imprecise language?

Clearly, wars and severe depressions sometimes promote union growth by fostering developments which, for example, raise the cost of living or make it easier for unions to obtain recognition and negotiating rights from employers. But these *ad hoc* 'disasters' are not themselves the 'causes' of union growth: the real determinants are the more fundamental and systematic factors, such as rising prices and union recognition, which are sometimes stimulated or at least facilitated by wars and depressions.[39]

---

38. *op. cit.*, 68.
39. Rezler, *op. cit.*, 8, made a similar point in noting that 'it was the philosophy and practice of the Democratic administrations and their receptive attitude toward unionism which primarily accounted for the spectacular growth of the unions during the two world wars and the Great Depression and not the wars and the Depression themselves.' But the existence of a Democratic administration is also an *ad hoc* factor which does not in itself 'cause' union

The force of these criticisms is strengthened by the failure of Dunlop and Bernstein to demonstrate that union growth is congruent in a very exact way with periods of war or of social unrest following a severe depression. They attributed the large increase in union membership around the turn of the century to the depression of 1893 and to the three-month Spanish-American War of 1898. But, as Rezler has pointed out, the 1893 depression is separated from the 1897—1903 period of union growth by a full business cycle,[40] and the increase in union membership began more than a year before the war started and continued for five years after it had ended. Similarly, the increase in union membership began several years before the Second World War started and stopped about a year before it ended, while the increase in union membership did not begin until the second year of the First World War and continued for two years after it had ended. Finally, although union membership expanded most dramatically in the periods identified by Dunlop and Bernstein, it nevertheless grew significantly in years such as 1907, 1910—13, and 1947. No war or severe depression occurred during these years, and neither Dunlop nor Bernstein offers any explanation for this growth in union membership.

A final criticism which may be directed against Dunlop and Bernstein is that although they stressed the multi-causal nature of union growth and offered a longer list of determinants than had previous writers, their analysis is nevertheless incomplete. In fact, Shister has claimed that it is incomplete in two respects: first, it omits certain important determinants and, second, some of those which are included are not 'sufficiently refined for operational purposes'.[41] In an attempt to overcome these deficiencies, Shister put forward his own framework for the analysis of union growth.

Of all the frameworks which have been advanced for analysing union growth, Shister's is the most complete in that it contains the largest number of variables, and it is the most systematic in that it explicitly specifies the interrelationships among them. Although it contains only

---

growth. Moreover, it need not even be connected with significant union growth as the periods 1945—52 and 1960—68 indicate. Hence without wishing to deny that Democratic administrations have sometimes facilitated union recognition, it seems better to stress the latter factor rather than the former.

40. 'The downturn in business activity which began in early 1893 reached its trough in June 1894. It was followed by a new cycle that surged to its peak in December 1895 and reached its depth in June 1897.' Rezler based this statement on the analysis of business cycles undertaken by the Cleveland Trust Company. See *op. cit.*, 5.

41. Joseph Shister, 'The Logic of Union Growth', *Journal of Political Economy*, LXI (October 1953), 413—33.

three major determinants – the work environment, the socio-legal framework, and trade union leadership – each of these is divided into numerous factors and sub-factors which are woven together into a coherent structure. Since several of these factors are more relevant to the explanation of disaggregate than of aggregate patterns of union growth,[42] and others have already been mentioned by previous writers,[43] they will not be discussed here. In fact, the only aspect of Shister's analytical framework which really needs attention here is trade union leadership.

Although previous writers such as Davis and Bernstein had mentioned the role of trade union leadership as a factor in union growth, Shister placed the most emphasis upon it and dealt with it at greatest length. He claimed that union leaders have an impact upon union growth through the organizing techniques which they devise for recruiting employees, the structural and governmental forms which they design for the union, and the nature of the collective bargaining relationships which they forge with employers and governments. And, in his view, their skill consists in an ability to recognize new conditions, to devise new policies in the above areas to meet these conditions, and to persuade the rank and file to pursue such policies.

Few people would quarrel with Shister's basic contention that union leadership has an impact upon union growth. Leadership is obviously an important factor in the exact timing of the emergence of a union. And its importance for 'the *union* incidence of growth – that is, which union succeeds in organizing a given group of workers – is', as Shister has pointed out, 'too obvious to need comment'.

But what is the role of leadership in aggregate union growth? Shister felt that the clue to answering this question is given by the characteristics of aggregate growth: it occurs in 'spurts', and during these spurts membership spreads from sector to sector rather than advancing in all sectors simultaneously and at the same pace. He claimed that these characteristics are partly determined by the nature of union leadership. Granted that the leading growth sector is 'virgin territory', he argued that the leadership in this sector cannot safely use traditional techniques but must display 'innovating ability'. Indeed, he

---

42. These include the 'technical and marketing contours' of particular industries; the composition of the labour force in particular industries in terms of sex, age, education, and race; and the degree of proximity between various work groups.

43. These include occupational mobility, cyclical variations in employment, and the socio-legal framework. Shister generally specified the relationship between these variables and union growth in a different way from previous writers.

likened the union leader in the lead sector to Schumpeter's entrepreneur.[44] 'Just as Schumpeter's innovating business leader successfully introduces into the economy new production functions . . . , so the innovating or creative union leader can be said to introduce successfully new "union-growth functions".' In the same way that Schumpeter's entrepreneur has followers, so the techniques and policies of the innovating union leader are soon imitated by those in other sectors. And 'just as the "swarm-like appearance of entrepreneurs" contributes to the cyclical pattern of economic growth, so too the swarmlike appearance of union leaders contributes to the spurtlike pattern of aggregative union growth.'

Shister presented no evidence whatsoever to support this theory of union leadership. Instead, he based his case entirely upon reasoning which had originally been devised to explain the behaviour of businessmen. This reasoning leaves a number of questions unanswered. Why is it that innovating union leaders appear at certain critical moments in the development of the labour movement? Given that such leaders emerge for whatever reason, what exactly are these revolutionary techniques which prove so successful in recruiting members? And whatever they may be, why are trade union leaders – a group renowned for its innate conservatism and well-defined sense of tradition on organizational matters – so quickly prepared to become a herd of imitators? Before the theory can be accepted even on *a priori* grounds, such questions must be answered. And before the theory can be accepted as a reasonable approximation of reality, some corroborative evidence must be presented on the nature of the recruitment process and the behaviour of union leaders.

Regardless of how union leaders behave, their role in aggregate union growth is fairly tightly circumscribed. For, as Shister himself has emphasized, 'union leaders can influence union growth only within limits, these limits being set by the relevant work environment and the sociolegal framework.' He pointed out, for example, that although John L. Lewis was an innovating union leader, he could do relatively little during the 1920s to organize the coal and other mass-production industries 'precisely because of the economic and institutional obstacles involved'.[45] And although Shister did not say so, there would probably have been a large-scale expansion of unionism in the United States once these obstacles were removed during the 1930s even if John L. Lewis had not existed. For this was a period in which favourable socioeconomic forces caused the labour movements of many Western

---

44. See Joseph A. Schumpeter, *The Theory of Economic Development* (Cambridge, Mass.: Harvard University Press, 1934).
45. *op. cit.*, 432.

countries to expand rapidly. In short, union leadership is dependent upon and constrained by the same socio-economic forces which motivate or enable workers to join trade unions. As such, it is very much a secondary and derivative determinant of aggregate union growth.

## Conclusion

The debate over the growth of aggregate unionism began shortly after the turn of the century, and it has continued until the present day. A great deal more has been written on the topic since Dunlop, Bernstein, and Shister wrote in the late 1940s and early 1950s,[46] but little that is new has been added over the past two decades. Indeed it is not too much to claim that few significant ideas have been contributed to the debate since Davis wrote in 1941.

Later writers such as Bernstein have drawn a sharp distinction between their own 'pluralistic' or multi-causal approach to union growth and what they regarded as the monistic approach of earlier writers such as Commons who stressed the importance of the business cycle. But, as has already been made clear, such a sharp contrast is unwarranted. For later writers such as Dunlop and Bernstein relied very heavily upon the explanatory power of the business cycle theory in certain historical contexts; indeed, in those very historical contexts in which most of the growth in American unionism has occurred. Moreover, the early theorists were not monists: most of them pointed out that factors other than the business cycle were also important determinants of union growth, and some, such as Weyforth and Davis, wrote about these factors at considerable length. It is true that the later writers added a few more variables to the list of possible determinants, a somewhat mixed blessing as is argued below; discussed some of the variables at greater length; and, in the case of Shister at least, ordered them in a more systematic fashion. But this hardly makes them

---

46. See, for example, the symposium in the *Annals of the American Academy of Social and Political Science*, CCCL (November 1963); and Solomon Barkin, *The Decline of the Labor Movement and What Can be Done about it* (Santa Barbara: Center for the Study of Democratic Institutions, 1961). See also Bernstein, 'The Growth of American Unions, 1945–1960', *op. cit.*; Joseph Shister, 'The Direction of Unionism, 1947–1967: Thrust or Drift?', *Industrial and Labor Relations Review*, XX (July 1967), 578–601; and Rezler, *op. cit.* For a review of the literature see Blum, *op. cit.*; and Woodrow L. Ginsburg, 'Union Growth, Government and Structure', *A Review of Industrial Relations Research*, ed. G. Somers (Madison: Industrial Relations Research Association, 1970), 207–60.

different in kind from the earlier theorists. At most, it makes for differences of emphasis and of degree.

Not only has the debate over aggregate union growth not progressed significantly since 1941, in at least one respect it has regressed. Although the amount of statistical data relevant to the debate has steadily increased, the theories of the earlier writers tend to be empirically better grounded than those of the later writers. There was relatively little statistical evidence which the Wisconsin School could present to support their theory about the development of the American labour movement in the nineteenth century, but at least they used the data that were available. The lack of adequate statistics on union membership stimulated the Johns Hopkins School of Barnett and Wolman to pioneer in collecting such data, and it was upon the resulting statistical series that they based their generalizations about union growth. Weyforth, another member of the Johns Hopkins School, pioneered by using the index of pig iron production as an indicator of business conditions and relating it to the growth of union membership. In verifying his theory, Davis used all the union membership and price data which were available not only for the United States but also for Britain, France, and Germany. Given that Weyforth and Davis were writing before it was commonplace in economics to use sophisticated statistical techniques for analysing empirical data, they gave a most impressive demonstration of the relationship between economic conditions and union growth.[47]

In contrast, although Dunlop generalized about the development of the American labour movement in both the nineteenth and twentieth centuries, he did not cite more empirical evidence than Commons and his associates had several decades earlier, if as much. He produced no data whatsoever to sustain his claim about the existence of Kondratieff cycles, and, as Shister pointed out, many of Dunlop's determinants were insufficiently refined for operational purposes. While Shister made many of these determinants more operational by dissecting them into their constituent elements, he advanced very little evidence of any kind to demonstrate that they actually were related to union growth in the way that he suggested. And although Bernstein assembled a considerable quantity of data for the United States and assessed it by means of a simple correlation technique, his statistical analysis was not exhaustive or rigorous. In fact, he had doubts as to the appropriateness

47. It is surprising that later writers have paid so little attention to the work of Weyforth and Davis because their work probably represents in theoretical and statistical terms the high points of the debate. It is also unfortunate because it is largely by ignoring them that writers such as Bernstein have been led to dismiss the early theorists as monists and to claim that the business cycle theory is without general validity.

of using quantitative techniques to study union growth, and employed them only because he felt they led to the same conclusions as more qualitative methods.[48] Like Dunlop, he preferred to rely upon a fairly subjective assessment of developments within a few critical periods rather than to undertake a more systematic quantitative analysis.

The result is that relatively little is really known about the determinants of union growth. It is true that a lengthy list of determinants has been assembled: the cost of living, unemployment, the attitude of employers, the legal framework and the institutions which devise and administer it, the growth and composition of the labour force, public opinion and the value system of the community, the rate of social mobility, union security provisions, and the quality of union leadership. But it is precisely the length of the list which is the problem. For although almost all the conceivable determinants have been listed, very little indication has been given of their relative importance. Indeed, it has not even been clearly demonstrated that all the factors which have been listed actually are determinants of aggregate union growth.

If the determinants of union growth are to be more firmly established, then greater use will have to made of statistical data and statistical methods. This is not meant to imply that this field of inquiry readily lends itself to such methods. It does not. For although union growth itself is quantifiable, many of the factors which might explain it are not. But at least some of them are, and considerable progress can be made if the relationship between these factors and union growth is analysed with the aid of econometric techniques. As Chapter 3 indicates, certain scholars have already begun to demonstrate the truth of this statement.

---

48. See 'The Growth of American Unions', *op. cit.*, 302; and his reply in the *American Economic Review, op. cit.*, 393.

# 3
# Models of Union Growth

Although no new significant ideas have been contributed to the theory of aggregate union growth for at least two decades, some progress has been made over the past few years in testing the theoretical notions which already exist.[1] Social scientists in Britain, the United States, and Australia have recently begun to develop econometric models of union growth which encompass many of the explanatory variables put forward by the theorists discussed in the previous chapter.[2] These models specify the individual variables more precisely and operationally, and thereby enable firmer conclusions to be drawn as to their relative importance.

## The Hines Model

The first contribution to the econometrics of union growth was made by Hines[3] in the context of the debate about the ability of trade unions to influence wages independently of the state of demand for labour.[4]

1. In addition to the work described here, there have also been attempts to test some of the theoretical notions discussed in the previous chapter by examining the determinants of 'new union organizing'. See Joseph Krislov, 'Union Organizing of New Units, 1955–1966', *Industrial and Labor Relations Review*, XXI (October 1967), 31–9; *idem*, 'Union Organizing and the Business Cycle, 1949–1966', *Southern Economic Journal*, XXVI (October 1966), 185–8; and *idem*, 'Organizing, Union Growth, and the Cycle, 1949–1966', *Labor History*, XI (Spring 1970), 212–22. See also n. 41.
2. Since the empirical work for this monograph was completed, a further econometric model of union growth has been constructed. See R. Swidinsky, 'Trade Union Growth in Canada, 1911–1970', *Relations Industrielles*, XXIX, no. 3 (1974), 435–51.
3. A. G. Hines, 'Trade Unions and Wage Inflation in the United Kingdom, 1893–1961', *Review of Economic Studies*, XXXI (October 1964), 221–52.
4. A good deal of this debate is summarized in C. Mulvey and J. A. Trevithick, 'Trade Unions and Wage Inflation', *Economic and Social Review*, IV (January 1973), 209–29.

His primary concern was to demonstrate that union power or 'pushfulness' as measured by the proportion of the labour force unionized is a major determinant of money wage rates. But because of the possibility of interdependence between the different variables, he built a simultaneous model which contains equations for the rate of change of wages, prices, and unionization. The following discussion will focus on the equation specifying the determinants of unionization.

Hines begins his discussion of the factors determining the rate of change of union density $(\Delta D)$[5] at the aggregate level by examining to what extent it is affected by the state of demand for labour as measured by the level of unemployment $(U)$ and/or the rate of change of unemployment $(\Delta U)$. He uses the ordinary least squares regression technique to fit the equation, $\Delta D_t = a + bU_t + c\Delta U_t$, to data for the period 1893–1961 and a variety of sub-periods.[6] The best fit is obtained by assuming that the relationship holds with a zero time lag. He finds that $\Delta U$ is not significant in any of the time periods, and that $U$ makes a 'significant contribution' to the explanation of the variation in $\Delta D$ only in the sub-period 1893–1912.[7] He also uses the Dicks–Mireaux and Dow index of excess demand as well as the deviation of the index of industrial production from a straight line trend as measures of the excess demand for labour, but finds that they do not produce any better results. In addition, he regresses $D$ (as opposed to $\Delta D$) upon $U$, and finds that the correlation between these two variables is also very poor. Hence he concludes that unionization is not significantly affected by the amount of excess demand for labour in the economy.

As part of an attempt to discover the direction of causality between unionization and the rate of change of money wage rates $(\Delta W)$, Hines postulates that the rate of change of union density is explained by the lagged rate of change of money wages, that is $\Delta D_t = f(\Delta W_{t-\alpha})$. He suggests that this relationship may hold because workers attribute wage rises to the efforts of unions and join them 'as a reward for services which they believe the unions have rendered', or because wage rises enable workers to afford the cost of union membership.[8] He tests the relationship with $\alpha$ = one year and $\alpha$ = six months, but finds that the

---

5. Hines specifies $\Delta D$ as the annual absolute difference, $D_t - D_{t-1}$. The exact specification of all his variables is given *op. cit.*, 243.
6. The exact periods are 1893–1912; 1921–38; 1949–61; 1921–38 and 1949–61; and 1893–1912, 1921–38, and 1949–61.
7. In fact, the estimated coefficient of $U$ is significantly different from zero not only for the period 1893–1912 but also for the overall period (1893–1912, 1921–38 and 1949–61) where it has an estimated '$t$' value of $-2.4606$. See *op. cit.*, 234.
8. *op. cit.*, 234–5.

resulting correlations are 'very poor'. Hence on the basis of Hines's results, lagged wage rates do not appear to be a significant determinant of union density.

Having disposed of these preliminaries, Hines puts forward the following unionization equation:

$$\Delta D_t = c_0 + c_1 D_{t-1} + c_2 \Delta P_{t-\frac{1}{2}} + c_3 Z_{t-\frac{1}{2}} + \epsilon_t$$

where $\epsilon$ is a random disturbance term and the expected signs are negative for $c_1$ and positive for $c_2$ and $c_3$. Hines's justification for including the level of unionization ($D$) is that there is an upper limit to the extent of unionization and the more closely this limit is approached, the more difficult it is to increase $D$ any further. $D$ is lagged a year in order to avoid introducing an element of spurious correlation with $\Delta D$.[9] The rate of change of retail prices ($\Delta P$) is included on the grounds that 'changes in the cost of living between wage settlements are a factor which influences the militancy of the unions and are therefore reflected in the rate of change of union membership.' The lag of six months is chosen to allow for behavioural delays. The level of real profits ($Z$) is claimed to be a good index of the prosperity of industry which, according to Kaldor whom Hines cites, 'determines both the eagerness of labour unions to demand higher wages and the ability of employers to grant them'.[10] After experimenting with the data, Hines decides that a six-month time lag for profits is the most appropriate.

The above equation was first estimated by means of ordinary least squares (OLS) for the period 1893–1961 and each of the sub-periods. It was then estimated by means of two-stage least squares (2SLS) for the period 1921–61 (excluding the war years) as part of an interdependent system which also included a price and wage equation.[11] The postulated six-month lag in the adjustment of unionization to prices is approximated in the simultaneous model by $\Delta P_t$ and $\Delta P_{t-1}$. The results are given in Table 3.1.

They suggest that $D_{t-1}$ is an important determinant of $\Delta D_t$. It is significant when estimated by two-stage least squares,[12] it is also

9. See Hines, *op. cit.*, 238 for a fuller explanation of this point.
10. N. Kaldor, 'Economic Growth and the Problem of Inflation', *Economica* (November 1959), 293.
11. In estimating the simultaneous model, the period 1893–1912 was excluded because of the difficulty of obtaining satisfactory data for some of the variables that enter into the price equation. Similarly, no estimates were made for the various sub-periods because the observations were too few in relation to the number of variables.
12. It should be noted that using '$t$' tests to test for the significance of the coefficients estimated by two-stage least squares is not adequate. The estimated standard errors are asymptotic, and the '$t$' test is a small sample test.

TABLE 3.1

HINES'S DETERMINANTS OF THE RATE OF CHANGE OF UNION DENSITY IN THE UNITED KINGDOM, 1893–1961

| Period | Constant | $D_{t-1}$ | $\Delta P_{t-\frac{1}{2}}$ | $\Delta P_t$ | $\Delta P_{t-1}$ | $Z_{t-\frac{1}{2}}$ | $\bar{R}^2$ | DW |
|---|---|---|---|---|---|---|---|---|
| OLS 1893–1912 | −1.5636 | −0.2235 (0.1935) | 0.0401 (0.0831) | | | 0.1039 (0.0482) | 0.2684 | 1.58[a] |
| OLS 1921–38 | 7.2845 | −0.2649 (0.1193) | 0.1919 (0.1006) | | | −0.0065 (0.0339) | 0.7948 | 1.22[b] |
| OLS 1949–61 | 30.5150 | −0.7938 (0.3416) | 0.0608 (0.0428) | | | 0.0095 (0.0096) | 0.5168 | 2.70[a] |
| OLS 1921–38 and 1949–61 | 4.1159 | −0.0881 (0.0357) | 0.3239 (0.0414) | | | −0.0161 (0.0207) | 0.6684 | 1.57[a] |
| OLS 1893–1912, 1921–38 and 1949–61 | 0.9316 | −0.1009 (0.0268) | 0.2887 (0.0364) | | | 0.0148 (0.0109) | 0.6175 | 1.63[a] |
| 2SLS 1921–38 and 1949–61 | 1.4014 | −0.1145 (0.0083) | | 0.4664 (0.0148) | −0.0978 (0.0129) | 0.0149 (0.0048) | 0.9843[c] | 1.31[bc] |

NOTES: Estimated standard errors of the estimated regression coefficients are in parentheses; those for the 2SLS estimates are asymptotic.

DW is the Durbin–Watson statistic, a measure of the first order serial correlation (autocorrelation) in the estimated residuals.

a. Indicates that the test showed no autocorrelation at the 1 per cent probability level.

b. Indicates that the test was inconclusive.

c. $\bar{R}^2$ for the equation estimated by 2SLS is not an adequate measure for the explanatory power of the simultaneous equation. Similarly, the DW test for autocorrelation is not an adequate test in a simultaneous equation system.

significant in all periods except 1893–1912 when estimated by ordinary least squares, and it has the correct sign in all cases. When estimated by ordinary least squares, $\Delta P_{t-\frac{1}{2}}$ has the correct sign and is significant in the overall period as well as in the shorter period 1921–38 and 1949–61. But it is not significant in the other three sub-periods. When estimated by two-stage least squares, $\Delta P_t$ and $\Delta P_{t-1}$ are both highly significant, but $\Delta P_{t-1}$ has the incorrect sign. Hence Hines concludes that prices have an important 'immediate effect' on $\Delta D$. The sign of $Z_{t-\frac{1}{2}}$ changes from one period to another when estimated by ordinary least squares; in fact, it is significant with the correct sign only in the period 1893–1912. When estimated by two-stage least squares, it has the correct sign and is significant, but, as Hines notes, 'its effect seems to be very small.'[13]

Hines carried his work a step further in 1969 by testing his wage inflation hypothesis at the disaggregated level.[14] He puts forward the following equation:

$$\Delta D_t = a_0 + a_1 D_{t-1} + a_2 Z_{t-1} + a_3 U_t + a_4 \Delta U_t + \epsilon_t$$

where $\epsilon$ is a random disturbance term and the expected signs are positive for $a_2$ and negative for $a_1$, $a_3$, and $a_4$. The zero lag on $U$ and $\Delta U$ and the one-year lag on $Z$ were chosen because they produced the 'best results'. The definition of each of the explanatory variables and the rationale for including them are generally the same as in the macro model. But whereas $Z$ was defined in the macro model as the level of real profits, it is specified in the disaggregated model as the ratio of profits to employee compensation.

Hines uses the ordinary least squares technique to fit the above equation to data for twelve broad industry groupings in the United Kingdom for the period 1948–62. He finds that on average the four explanatory variables account for 50 per cent of the variance in $\Delta D$. $D_{t-1}$ has the correct sign in ten of the twelve industries but is significant in only three industries. $Z_{t-1}$ has the correct sign in five industries but is significant in only two industries. The $U$ coefficient has the correct sign in three industries and is insignificant in all cases. The $\Delta U$ coefficient has the correct sign in ten industries but is significant in

13. *op. cit.*, 242.
14. 'Wage Inflation in the United Kingdom, 1948–62: A Disaggregated Study', *Economic Journal*, LXXIX (March 1969), 66–89. He also carried his work forward in 'Unemployment and the Rate of Change of Money Wage Rates in the United Kingdom, 1862–1963: A Reappraisal', *Review of Economics and Statistics* (February 1968), 60–67. But since this paper is concerned with specifying and testing a wage rather than a unionization equation, it is not discussed here.

only two instances. When the simple regression between $\Delta D$ and $U$ is examined, the regression coefficient is significant in four cases. Similar results are obtained when Hines postulates a Koyck-type distributed lag in the relationship between these two variables.[15] He also notes that the pattern of the results is not affected by replacing the linear form of the unemployment variable with the non-linear form suggested by the Phillips curve. He concludes from this analysis that although unemployment makes some contribution to explaining $\Delta D$, it is not the 'dominant factor'.

Hines then decides to see whether aggregate phenomena influence the rate of change of unionization in each industry. The variables selected for analysis are the aggregate level of unemployment, the aggregate rate of change of unionization, and the rate of change of retail prices. He finds that the 'performance of unemployment was again disappointing', and that 'changes in the cost of living appeared to be the most important of these variables'.

He concludes that on balance a 'considerable proportion' of the variance in unionization is accounted for by 'the level of unemployment, the level of unionisation itself, the ratio of profits to employee compensation, as well as by aggregate phenomena, such as changes in the cost of living'. But he feels 'it is worthy of note that for the functional forms and alternative lag specifications which were tried the contribution made by unemployment is not as substantial as might have been expected if unemployment were the dominant influence' on union density. He also observes that 'a part of the variance in the unionisation variable may be accounted for by socio-political factors which are usually regarded as exogeneous in economic models.'[16]

Hines's model has been subjected to considerable criticism. Purdy and Zis claim that it is 'theoretically weak, being based on no more than *ad hoc* rationalisations of empirical associations', and that many of these rationalizations are extremely dubious.[17] Thomas and Stoney have shown that considered as a stochastic difference equation system, the Hines model is dynamically explosive.[18] And Godfrey has argued that this property makes it difficult to interpret Hines's original

15. That is, he postulates that the rate of change of unionization in a given period is a weighted average of all past levels of unemployment, the weights declining exponentially.
16. 'Wage Inflation in the United Kingdom, 1948–62', *op. cit.*, 82–3.
17. D. L. Purdy and G. Zis, 'Trade Unions and Wage Inflation in the UK: A Reappraisal', *Essays in Modern Economics*, ed. Michael Parkin and A. R. Nobay (London: Longman, 1973), 322.
18. R. L. Thomas and P. J. M. Stoney, 'A Note on the Dynamic Properties of the Hines Inflation Model', *Review of Economic Studies*, XXXVII (April 1970), 286–94.

estimates and suggests that the model may be misspecified.[19] But these theoretical and methodological deficiencies in Hines's work pertain primarily to his simultaneous system as a whole and, in particular, to his argument concerning the determination of money wage rates. They only indirectly affect his unionization equation.[20]

This is not the case, however, with the statistical shortcomings which characterize his work. His aggregate unemployment series relates to the United Kingdom for the period 1892–1939 but to Great Britain for the years 1948–61. Moreover, he adds 20 per cent to the post-1948 figures to compensate for changes in coverage brought about by the 1948 National Insurance Act, but he offers no justification for the magnitude of this figure. And given that the scope of the national insurance legislation was increased on several occasions between 1911 and 1948, it is difficult to understand why he only adjusts the post-1948 figures. In addition, he uses the GDP price deflator to compute $\Delta P$ for the years 1921–58 supplemented by the retail price index for 1959–61, whereas it would have been more consistent to use the retail price–cost of living index for the whole period. In calculating his aggregate union density series, he uses United Kingdom membership data but Great Britain labour force data, and the latter include groups such as employers, the self-employed, and the armed forces, which are outside the scope of trade unionism.[21] Finally, the disaggregated density series which he uses are so notoriously unreliable that it would be extremely rash to place any faith in the equations which are based upon them.[22]

19. Leslie Godfrey, 'The Phillips Curve: Incomes Policy and Trade Union Effects', *The Current Inflation*, ed. H. G. Johnson and A. R. Nobay (London: Macmillan, 1971), 112–13.

20. One methodological deficiency which does directly affect his unionization equation, however, is that in calculating the coefficient of determination in his two-stage least squares results he incorrectly uses the actual rather than the instrumental variables. When calculated correctly, the coefficient of determination given by the two-stage least squares procedure can never be higher than that given by the ordinary least squares procedure. This means that the 'fit' for the unionization equation must at most be 67 per cent instead of the 98 per cent reported.

21. On this point see Purdy and Zis, *op. cit.*, 299–303 and D. Dogas and A. G. Hines, 'Trade Unions and Wage Inflation in the UK: A Critique of Purdy and Zis', *Applied Economics*, VII (September 1975), 201–9.

22. The problem is that the Department of Employment does not distribute the membership of the two major general unions by industry. Consequently, Hines allocates their *total* membership to a very small group of industries in which he claims the bulk of their membership lies. This is clearly unsound since these two unions have large numbers of members in virtually every industry. There is an additional problem. In preparing its industrial analysis of union membership, the Department of Employment allocates the total membership of a union to the industry in which the majority of its members are deemed to be employed. In the case of industrial unions such as the

32

The empirical weaknesses in Hines's work limit the significance which can be attached to his findings. These are, in any case, only marginally and indirectly concerned with the question of what determines union growth. Indeed, his model does not even attempt to deal with the two periods – 1913–20 and 1939–48 – in which union density in the United Kingdom increased most rapidly. For a more substantial and direct attempt to isolate the determinants of aggregate union growth, attention must be directed to the work of Ashenfelter and Pencavel.

## The Ashenfelter and Pencavel Model

Ashenfelter and Pencavel's model links the growth of union membership in the United States between 1900 and 1960 to a set of economic, social, and political variables.[23] Their basic equation is

$$\Delta T_t = \beta_0 + \beta_1 \Delta P_t + \sum_{i=0}^{N} \beta_{2i} \Delta E^*_{t-i} + \beta_3 g(U^P_t, t - \theta) + \beta_4 (T/E^*)_{t-1}$$
$$+ \beta_5 G_t + \epsilon_t$$

where $\Delta T$ is the annual percentage change in trade union membership, $\epsilon$ is a random disturbance term, and the expected signs of all the coefficients are positive except that of $\beta_4$. The nature of the explanatory variables can best be explained by discussing them in turn.

$\Delta P$ is the annual percentage rate of change of consumer prices. It is included in the model on the grounds that 'the difference between the expected rate of change of the worker's money wages, as based on the immediate past, and the actual rate of change of money wages is likely to be greatest when consumer prices are increasing rapidly.' Indeed, 'in this situation the rate of change of the worker's real wages declines and may even become negative so that his desire to organize in order to maintain his real wages is highest.'[24]

---

National Union of Mineworkers, this procedure involves little error. But most unions in Britain span several occupations and industries (e.g., the Amalgamated Union of Engineering Workers), and in such cases the Department's procedure involves considerable error. See G. S. Bain and R. J. Price, *Profiles of Union Growth* (Oxford: Blackwell, forthcoming) for a discussion of this problem and for an attempt to produce more accurate industrial density data for Great Britain.

23. Orley Ashenfelter and John H. Pencavel, 'American Trade Union Growth: 1900–1960', *Quarterly Journal of Economics*, LXXXIII (August 1969), 434–48.
24. *ibid.*, 436.

$\Delta E^*$ is the annual percentage rate of change of employment (excluding unemployment) in the 'unionizable' sectors of the economy.[25] Ashenfelter and Pencavel offer three reasons for including this variable in the model. First, 'a major cost of joining a union, employer retaliation, is likely to be lowest when the labor market is tightening.' Second, 'the trouble and inconvenience incurred by a worker in joining a trade union is reduced when the union embarks on membership drives' and 'a period of increasing employment is favorable to successful organizing drives: the organizing funds of unions will be larger; and the potential union member is more receptive to organizing efforts.' Third, 'with the advent of union security agreements in more recent years, increases in employment often lead automatically to upturns in union membership.' Ashenfelter and Pencavel postulate a lag in the relationship between $\Delta T$ and $\Delta E^*$ on the assumption that 'workers are reluctant to leave unions immediately when employment is declining both because of social and political ties and for economic reasons', and also to allow for union membership figures which 'sometimes include as members workers who have temporarily stopped paying dues because they are unemployed'.[26]

Ashenfelter and Pencavel claim that workers have a 'stock of grievances' which cause them to be discontented and to join unions as a form of protest. They suggest that this stock of grievances or 'worker discontent' at any time is a function of the amount of unemployment in the preceding trough of the business cycle $(U_t^P)$.[27]

25. Ashenfelter and Pencavel define the 'unionized' sectors of employment as manufacturing, mining, construction, and transport and utilities. More than 80 per cent of total union membership was concentrated in these four sectors in 1960.
26. *ibid.*, 436–7. They assume that union growth depends upon a short moving average of previous rates of change of employment in the unionized sectors. They think it is 'reasonable to suppose that the response of union growth to changes in employment will be complete within three years, so the $\beta_{2i}$ have been estimated with $N$ set equal to 3'. In effect, this means that $\Sigma E_{t-i}^*$ ($i = 0,1,2,3$) represents four separate measures of the percentage rate of change of total employment in the unionized sectors of the economy: $E_t^*$, $E_{t-1}^*$, $E_{t-2}^*$, and $E_{t-3}^*$. See *ibid.*, 440, n. 8 for a more complete discussion of the procedure used to formulate and estimate the lag structure.
27. $U_t^P$ is a step function which takes on fifteen values in the period 1900–1960. 'In order to allow for the possibility that the effect on unionism of a given pool of grievances "decays" as time passes, the variable actually used is a function of $U_t^P$ and $t - \theta$, where "$t$" is the current year and $\theta$ is the year of the preceding trough in the business cycle.' The precise form which Ashenfelter and Pencavel specify for the function $g(U_t^P, t - \theta)$ is $\lambda^{(t-\theta)}U_t^P$ with $0 \leqslant \lambda \leqslant 1$. Thus when $U_t^P$ takes on a new value in the trough of a recession, $t - \theta = 0$ and $g(U_t^P, t - \theta)$, the measure of social discontent, is at its maximum. As the business cycle continues, however, $t - \theta$ increases monotonically so that $g(U_t^P, t - \theta)$, the measure of social discontent, 'decays'. In the actual estimation, however, Ashenfelter and Pencavel find

$(T/E^*)$ is total trade union membership as a percentage of 'unionizable' employment. This variable is included in the model on the grounds that 'the greater the proportion of employment in the union sectors that is already unionized the more difficult it is further to increase union membership.' The variable is lagged one period.[28]

The final explanatory variable in the Ashenfelter and Pencavel model is the percentage of Democrats in the United States House of Representatives $(G)$. They regard this variable as a proxy for the extent of 'pro-labor sentiment' which they claim determines not only people's responsiveness to union recruiting drives but also the amount of legislation favourable to union growth. They justify this index on the grounds that unions and their members generally tend to support the Democratic Party and hence the periods in which it predominates 'should reflect a high degree of pro-labor sentiment'.[29]

Ashenfelter and Pencavel first estimate the above equation by means of ordinary least squares (OLS) regression techniques. In addition, to allow for Hines's argument that $\Delta T$ and $\Delta P$ may be mutually dependent,[30] they obtain instrumental variable estimates (IV) of the above equation.[31] The results are given in Table 3.2 and they clearly

---

that the value of $\lambda$ which minimized the sum of squared residuals was in the interval $0.95 \leqslant \lambda \leqslant 1$. In other words, there is little evidence of a decay in the response of $\Delta T$ to $U_t^P$. Hence for the sake of simplicity they assume that $\lambda = 1$ in each of the equations. In short, $U_t^P$ is not allowed to decay. See *ibid.*, 440–41.

28. They also use the reciprocal of this variable $(T/E^*)_{t-1}^{-1}$ to test the non-linear variant of this hypothesis, namely that 'the difficulty of further organization increases more than proportionately with increases in the level of unionization'.

29. *ibid.*, 439.

30. In other words, to the extent that union growth has an effect on money wages, and the latter has an effect on prices, the direction of causation may be from $\Delta T$ to $\Delta P$ rather than from $\Delta P$ to $\Delta T$ as the model implies.

31. The instrument used for $\Delta P$ is an ordinary least squares linear combination of the unemployment rate, the percentage change in average labour productivity, and the lagged rate of change of money wages. See Ashenfelter and Pencavel, *op. cit.*, 441, n. 2.

The way in which Ashenfelter and Pencavel deal with the potential simultaneity problem is not entirely satisfactory. There is a contradiction in assuming that it is $W_{t-\theta}$ which affects $\Delta P_t$. For if this is the case, then there is no need to worry about simultaneity. For $\Delta W_{t-\theta}$ is a lagged jointly dependent variable, and as such it is a predetermined variable which does not give rise to simultaneity problems. However, if $\Delta W_t$ (as opposed to $\Delta W_{t-\theta}$) is the term which affects $\Delta P_t$, then the interdependence between $\Delta T_t$, $\Delta W_t$, and $\Delta P_t$ needs to be clearly specified and the system estimated by the simultaneous equation method. It is also important to note that although the OLS and IV techniques produce similar estimates, the estimated standard errors of the $\Delta P$ coefficients are doubled (and hence their '$t$' values are almost halved) when the IV method is used. The reason for this would seem to be that the instrument exhibits less variation than $\Delta P_t$, and hence may be more highly correlated with $\Delta E_t$ than the original $\Delta P_t$.

## TABLE 3.2

### ASHENFELTER AND PENCAVEL'S DETERMINANTS OF THE RATE OF CHANGE OF UNION MEMBERSHIP IN THE UNITED STATES, 1904—1960

| Period | Constant | $\Delta P_t$ | $\Delta E^\dagger_t$ | $\Delta E^*_{t-1}$ | $\Delta E^*_{t-2}$ | $\Delta E^*_{t-3}$ | $\Sigma_i \Delta E^*_{t-i}$ | $U^\dagger_t$ | $(T/E^*)_{t-1}$ | $(T/E^*)^{-1}_{t-1}$ | $G_t$ | $R^2$ | SEE | DW |
|---|---|---|---|---|---|---|---|---|---|---|---|---|---|---|
| OLS 1904—60 | -10.584 (-4.2235) | 0.673 (5.2578) | 0.127 (1.6076) | 0.110 (2.3404) | 0.083 (1.8863) | 0.047 (1.3824) | 0.367 (2.3376) | 0.249 (2.5938) | -0.063 (-2.3333) | | 0.222 (3.9643) | 0.749 | 3.74 | 1.66 |
| OLS 1904—60 | -15.322 (-5.0618) | 0.683 (5.3359) | 0.122 (1.5250) | 0.107 (2.2766) | 0.082 (1.8636) | 0.046 (1.3529) | 0.357 (2.2739) | 0.290 (3.0526) | | 69.170 (2.2220) | 0.216 (3.9273) | 0.749 | 3.74 | 1.68 |
| IV 1904—59 | -11.070 (-4.3395) | 0.614 (2.9519) | 0.150 (1.4563) | 0.119 (2.0169) | 0.084 (1.7872) | 0.044 (1.2941) | 0.397 (2.0255) | 0.220 (2.0561) | -0.055 (-1.9643) | | 0.230 (3.9655) | 0.751 | 3.74 | 1.62 |
| IV 1904—59 | -15.357 (-5.0467) | 0.622 (2.9761) | 0.145 (1.4078) | 0.117 (1.9831) | 0.083 (1.7660) | 0.044 (1.2941) | 0.389 (1.9746) | 0.256 (2.3704) | | 62.447 (1.9464) | 0.231 (4.0526) | 0.752 | 3.74 | 1.64 |

NOTES:  Figures in parentheses are estimated '$t$' values.
The coefficient of $\Sigma_i \Delta E^*_{t-i}$ is the sum of the estimated coefficients of all the $\Delta E^*$ terms with its standard error derived from the model's estimated variance–covariance matrix and '$t$' values are estimated from this information. But the variable $\Delta E^*_{t-i}$ obviously does not appear in the model for it is linearly dependent with $\Delta E^*_{t-i}$ ($i = 0, 1, 2, 3$).

support the hypotheses advanced by Ashenfelter and Pencavel.[32] The independent variables account for approximately 75 per cent of the variance in union growth. All the regression coefficients have the expected sign and, with the exception of the coefficients for $\Delta E_t^*$ and $\Delta E_{t-3}^*$, are significantly different from zero at either the 1 per cent or 5 per cent significance level. The linear and non-linear variants of $T/E^*$ 'perform almost equally well', and hence support the hypothesis that the 'further growth of unions is hampered by their own size'.[33] The difference between the ordinary least squares and the instrumental variable estimates of the $\Delta P$ coefficient is small, leading Ashenfelter and Pencavel to comment that 'the implication of this result is to reaffirm the evidence for a strong causal effect of price changes on union growth.' They also conclude, after examining the movements in the independent variables during four historically important sub-periods, that 'there is no consistent evidence in favor of amending the analysis to make special cases of these four periods.'[34] In short, they feel that 'a single behavioral relationship can explain the progress of the American labor movement in the twentieth century.'[35]

The Ashenfelter and Pencavel model clearly produces good results. It nevertheless has certain weaknesses. Ashenfelter and Pencavel themselves mention that measurement errors and the inability to quantify such strategic factors as the quality of union leadership 'limit the confidence that can be placed in the precise estimates presented'.[36] In addition, Mancke has offered several criticisms of the model.[37] Although Ashenfelter and Pencavel challenge his argument and claim it reveals a 'serious misunderstanding' of their model,[38] some of Mancke's criticisms are nevertheless justified. There are also other criticisms which can be advanced.

Mancke finds 'uninteresting' the fact that the coefficients of the $\Delta E^*$ terms, as estimated by Ashenfelter and Pencavel, are positive and considers that union security provisions render it 'nearly definitional' that 'if the percentage rate of change of total employment rises, *ceteris*

32. Ashenfelter and Pencavel also test the model using $\Delta D$ rather than $\Delta T$ as the dependent variable and find that although 'the results were not so good', the 'basic conclusions were unaltered' (*ibid.*, 440, n. 6).
33. However, the two formulations have different quantitative implications for future union growth. See *ibid.*, 444.
34. *ibid.*, 445–7. The four sub-periods are 1917–20, 1924–39, 1933–7, and 1941–5.
35. *ibid.*, 434.
36. *ibid.*, 447.
37. R. B. Mancke, 'American Trade Union Growth, 1900–1960: A Comment', *Quarterly Journal of Economics*, LXXXV (February 1971), 187–93.
38. 'American Trade Union Growth, 1900–1960: A Rejoinder', *Quarterly Journal of Economics*, LXXXVI (November 1972), 691–2.

*paribus*, the percentage rate of change of total union membership rises.'[39] Ashenfelter and Pencavel answer this criticism by pointing out that this is a hypothesis which they tested and rejected.[40] Moreover, their findings are supported by those of Adams and Krislov who tested the ability of the Ashenfelter and Pencavel model to explain an important component of union growth, 'new union organizing', which is not affected by union security provisions.[41]

But Mancke's criticism cannot be dismissed so easily. $\Delta E^*$ is measuring not one but three effects. First, there is the effect of changes in the rate of growth of potential membership which, other things being equal, might be expected to lead to equal proportionate changes in actual membership. Second, there is the effect of changes in the excess demand for labour or the degree of 'tightness' in the labour market which, in Ashenfelter and Pencavel's view, determines the ability of employers to oppose unionism and the ease with which unions can launch successful organizing drives. Third, there is the effect of changes in the distribution of employment between high and low density sectors of the labour force. While it is reasonable to expect that all these effects will be positively related to union growth, there is no reason to expect that they will all be of the same magnitude. Hence it is quite conceivable that the magnitude of the first effect is unity, but that the overall effect is less than this because the magnitude of the second and third effects is less than unity.[42] In other words, the test

39. *op. cit.*, 188–9. He adds that this positive relationship is enhanced by Ashenfelter and Pencavel defining $E^*$ to cover only the 'unionizable' sectors of employment.

40. Ashenfelter and Pencavel claim that if a given change in unionizable employment automatically led to the same increase in union membership, then the sum of the coefficients on the $\Delta E^*_{t-i}$ would not differ significantly from unity. In fact, as estimated by Ashenfelter and Pencavel, the sum of the coefficients on the $\Delta E^*_{t-i}$ is about 0.4, indicating that some 40 per cent of employment changes in the unionized sectors over a three-year period are reflected, *ceteris paribus*, in proportionate changes in union membership. See Ashenfelter and Pencavel (1969), *op. cit.*, 444, n. 6. See also below, pp. 42 and 44.

41. Arvil V. Adams and Joseph Krislov, 'New Union Organizing: A Test of the Ashenfelter–Pencavel Model of Trade Union Growth', *Quarterly Journal of Economics*, LXXXVII (May 1974), 310–11. 'New union organizing' is measured by the number of voters in previously unorganized bargaining units which selected union representation in any given year between 1949 and 1970 in elections supervised by the National Labor Relations Board.

42. This argument can be expressed more precisely in mathematical form. Using $E$ to denote total employment, it is tautological that $E^* = E \cdot E^*/E$. And since $E = L - uL$ where $L$ is the labour force and $u$ is the percentage of unemployment, then by substitution $E^* = (1 - u)L \cdot E^*/E$. Hence

$$dE^* = (LE^*/E)d(1 - u) + (1 - u)(E^*/E)dL + (1 - u)Ld(E^*/E),$$

implying that the coefficient of $dE^*$ is a combined effect of three separate

which Ashenfelter and Pencavel use to rebut Mancke's criticism is not valid. For his definitional argument would imply an employment coefficient of unity, only if the regressor was total employment as opposed to employment in the unionized sectors.[43]

Given that there are three separate employment effects, it is surprising that Ashenfelter and Pencavel tried to capture them all by using the single variable $\Delta E^*$. For this makes it impossible to distinguish between the various effects, and, in addition, some of them can be more appropriately measured by other variables. For example, in as much as the objective is to measure the extent to which unions are able to launch successful organizing drives and the extent to which employers are able to oppose these drives, unemployment is a more appropriate measure of these factors than $\Delta E^*$. For $\Delta E^*$ only refers to the highly unionized sectors of the economy – increasingly those sectors in which unions are least likely to launch organizing drives and in which employers are least likely to oppose unionism – whereas the unemployment rate refers to all sectors of employment. In short, given Ashenfelter and Pencavel's argument, it is surprising that they did not introduce the annual level and/or rate of change of unemployment into their model instead of, or in addition to, $\Delta E^*$.

In so far as the unemployment rate enters the model, it does so as a step function of the rate at the preceding trough of the business cycle ($U^P$). But Ashenfelter and Pencavel do not intend $U^P$ to be a measure of unemployment as such. Rather, they put it forward as an index of 'labor's stock of grievances'. It is meant to capture the essence of the argument advanced by writers such as Bernstein that 'a severe and

---

effects: $d(1-u)$ is the effect of changes in the excess demand for labour, $dL$ is the effect of changes in the rate of growth of potential membership, and $E^*/E$ is the effect of changes in the relative importance of the highly unionized sectors of employment. This means that Ashenfelter and Pencavel's basic equation may be written as

$$\Delta T_t = \beta_0 + \beta_1 \Delta L_t + \beta_2 \Delta(1-u)_t + \beta_3 \Delta(E^*/E)_t + \beta_4 X + \epsilon_t$$

where X is a vector of all the other specified variables. Obviously, the coefficient of the $\Delta E^*$ terms, as estimated by Ashenfelter and Pencavel, is an average of $\beta_1$, $\beta_2$, and $\beta_3$. Hence even if $\beta_1 = 1$, if $\beta_2$ and $\beta_3 < 1$, then the overall average will be less than unity.

The coefficients on $\Delta E^*$ may also be accounted for by certain methodological problems associated with the Ashenfelter and Pencavel model. See below, p. 44, n. 55.

43. It is interesting that when Sharpe used total employment as a regressor he obtained a coefficient not significantly different from unity, but that when he used employment in the unionized sectors, he obtained a coefficient similar to that of Ashenfelter and Pencavel. See Ian G. Sharpe, 'The Growth of Australian Trade Unions: 1907–1969', *Journal of Industrial Relations*, XIII (June 1971), 144 and 153, n. 15.

prolonged depression imposes heavy burdens upon workers and their families, causing them to develop sharp grievances against the existing social order,' and 'this, in turn, makes them prone to affiliate with instrumentalities of protest, including unions.'[44] Hence $U^P$ is open to all the criticisms which the previous chapter raised against Bernstein's argument.[45] In particular, what exactly are these grievances and by what process do they result in workers joining trade unions? Do they represent anything more than dissatisfaction with rising prices and falling employment, factors which are already taken into account in the model by the inclusion of the variables $\Delta P$ and $\Delta E^*$? If they do, then why are these additional factors which cause 'worker discontent' not spelt out more precisely? In short, as specified by Ashenfelter and Pencavel, $U^P$ is simply a rag bag which may contain everything or nothing. As such, its effect is extremely difficult to interpret.

The variable $T/E$ * also poses a problem of interpretation. Ashenfelter and Pencavel argue that its coefficient should be negative because 'the greater the proportion of employment in the union sectors that is already unionized the more difficult it is further to increase union membership.'[46] But Mancke argues that while 'this assertion might be true after total union membership had exceeded some critical level', it is 'doubtful that it would be true when total union membership is very low'. Indeed, he feels that 'it is quite likely that in the early years of the twentieth century, when union membership was very low', a rise in $T/E$ * 'would have led to a reduction in the risk of being a union member and therefore to an increase rather than a decrease' in $\Delta T$. Because he thinks it 'implausible' that the true relationship between $T/E^*$ and $\Delta T$ has always been negative and linear, he suggests that it is merely 'coincidental' that the former variable has a significant negative coefficient.[47] In reply, Ashenfelter and Pencavel point out that both $T/E^*$ and its non-linear variant $(T/E^*)^{-1}$ were used in the regressions, and they perform almost equally well. But there are other non-linear forms such as the quadratic, and it may be that one of these would be more appropriate. The need to determine whether or not this is the case is underlined by the work of Adams and Krislov who found that both $T/E^*$ and $(T/E^*)^{-1}$ were insignificant and had the 'wrong' sign.[48]

There are also certain difficulties connected with the variable $G$, the proportion of Democrats in the United States House of Representa-

44. Irving Bernstein, 'The Growth of American Unions', *American Economic Review*, XLIV (June 1954), 316.
45. See p. 19 above.
46. *op. cit.*, 438.
47. *op. cit.*, 189.
48. *op. cit.*, 310.

tives. To begin with, the theoretical justification for the variable is not entirely satisfactory. Ashenfelter and Pencavel regard it as a proxy for the extent of 'pro-labor sentiment' which they claim determines people's responsiveness to union recruitment campaigns as well as the amount of legislation favourable to union growth. Without wishing to suggest that 'pro-labor sentiment' is inimicable to unionism, it is possible to question how relevant it is to the decision to join a union. It seems reasonable to suggest that people join unions not so much because a vague 'pro-labor' feeling generally prevails in society as because a specific need for unionism is felt in the work place. Similarly, the climate of opinion is no doubt linked to the legal framework, but the link is not as direct or as mechanistic as Ashenfelter and Pencavel suggest. Shister, for example, has offered several reasons why the two factors may diverge quite widely at least in the short run.[49]

Even granted for the moment that 'pro-labor sentiment' does significantly promote union growth and that the nature and magnitude of this sentiment can be captured by the strength of the Democratic Party, $G$ is specified too narrowly to be an adequate political index. For the Senate, the Presidency, and the judiciary also play a role in the legislative process, and their role is often more important than that of the House of Representatives. In addition, the United States is a federal country, and certain legislation which is important for union growth, such as right-to-work laws and laws relating to bargaining rights for public employees, is passed at state rather than national level. Hence before $G$ could be accepted as an adequate index of the Democratic Party's popular appeal or legislative influence, it would have to be specified in such a way as to reflect its strength not only in the United States House of Representatives, but also in these other institutions and levels of government.

But even if a wider and more representative index of Democratic strength were constructed, it would not be a good proxy for 'pro-labor sentiment'. Ashenfelter and Pencavel's claim to the contrary is based on the fact that unions and their members generally tend to support the Democratic Party. This is a circular argument: union growth is explained by Democratic strength, while Democratic strength is explained by union growth. Leaving aside this circularity, the fact that unions and their members generally support the Democratic Party hardly means that it reflects 'pro-labor sentiment'. For not all

49. Joseph Shister, 'The Logic of Union Growth', *Journal of Political Economy*, LXI (October 1953), 425–6. In addition, the climate of opinion in which unions operate and, in particular, their 'social acceptability' may be a consequence rather than a cause of union growth. See Julius Rezler, *Union Growth Reconsidered* (New York: Kossuth Foundation, 1961), 14–15.

Democrats are pro-labour; indeed, many, such as those from the South, are generally anti-labour. Even those who are pro-labour are not necessarily elected for this reason. Their views on labour questions, particularly those concerned with union growth, may have little saliency for rank-and-file unionists, let alone the non-unionists who make up the majority of the electorate. Perhaps this explains why the Democratic Party has not repealed the Taft-Hartley Act, in spite of the labour movement's insistence over the past twenty-five years that it is 'slave labor legislation' which, among other things, restricts union growth.

None of the above is meant to deny that the Democrats have on certain occasions and in certain contexts promoted union growth by, for example, passing legislation which facilitated union recognition. But there is no simple and fixed relationship between union growth and the strength of the Democratic Party. For just as there have been periods in which Democratic strength has been used to encourage union growth, so there have been other periods in which it has not. Whatever the relationship between $G$ and the political factor that Ashenfelter and Pencavel really desire to measure, surely, as Mancke has queried, it cannot have been constant and linear for 61 years.[50] This scepticism receives some confirmation from the tendency of the Ashenfelter and Pencavel model to overpredict the rate of change of union membership during the Democratic Party's congressional upsurge of 1954–60.[51] It receives further confirmation from Adams and Krislov's finding that $G$ is only marginally significant in explaining 'new union organizing' in the United States over the past two decades.[52]

Most of the above criticisms are concerned with the theoretical justification for the different variables and the way in which they are specified. There are also certain methodological problems associated with the Ashenfelter and Pencavel model. These can best be revealed by re-running their model using different combinations of the explanatory variables and analysing the contribution which each of these makes. The results are given in Table 3.3.

The dominant explanatory variable is clearly $\Delta P$. When introduced on its own in Regression 12, it produces a highly significant coefficient with the expected positive sign and a $\bar{R}^2$ of 36 per cent. Indeed, $\Delta P$ explains almost the same proportion of the variance in $\Delta T$ as the four regressors of $\Delta E_{t-i}^*$ taken together. It can be seen from Regression 3 that the coefficients of $\Delta E_{t-i}^*$ sum to 0.90.[53] The '$t$' test indicates

50. *op. cit.*, 190.
51. See Ashenfelter and Pencavel (1969), *op. cit.*, 435, figure 1.
52. *op. cit.*, 310.
53. See the discussion (above, pp. 38–9) about whether or not the sum of the coefficients of the $\Delta E^*$ regressors is unity.

TABLE 3.5

## A RE-RUN OF THE ASHENFELTER AND PENCAVEL MODEL OF AMERICAN UNION GROWTH, 1904–1960

| REGRESSION | 1 | 2 | 3 | 4 | 5 | 6 | 7 | 8 | 9 | 10 | 11 | 12 |
|---|---|---|---|---|---|---|---|---|---|---|---|---|
| **Summary Statistics** | | | | | | | | | | | | |
| $R^2$ | 0.7436 | 0.7436 | 0.3812 | 0.4563 | 0.6570 | 0.7201 | 0.1496 | 0.3036 | 0.3093 | 0.3206 | 0.3192 | 0.3684 |
| $\bar{R}^2$ | 0.7129 | 0.7128 | 0.3583 | 0.4255 | 0.6306 | 0.6927 | 0.1341 | 0.2909 | 0.2837 | 0.2821 | 0.2806 | 0.3569 |
| SEE | 3.80 | 3.80 | 5.68 | 5.38 | 4.31 | 3.93 | 6.60 | 5.97 | 6.01 | 6.01 | 6.02 | 5.69 |
| $F$ | 24.1764 | 24.1651 | 16.6336 | 14.8266 | 24.8954 | 26.2450 | 9.6738 | 23.9770 | 12.0904 | 8.3359 | 8.2816 | 32.0782 |
| $df$ | 6, 50 | 6, 50 | 2, 54 | 3, 53 | 4, 52 | 5, 51 | 1, 55 | 1, 55 | 2, 54 | 3, 53 | 3, 53 | 1, 55 |
| DW | 1.6216 | 1.6406 | 0.6941 | 0.7432 | 1.5038 | 1.4805 | 0.9206 | 0.8356 | 0.8703 | 0.8789 | 0.8797 | 0.6928 |
| **Estimated Coefficients** | | | | | | | | | | | | |
| Constant | −10.5898 (−4.1560) | −15.2315 (−4.9470) | 2.2418 (2.8507) | 1.7271 (2.2488) | −3.2843 (−2.9919) | −11.4407 (−4.4394) | −0.5542 (−0.3682) | −14.3522 (−3.8978) | −13.5051 (−3.4519) | −12.9183 (−3.3269) | −15.9353 (−3.3181) | 1.7488 (2.1879) |
| $\Delta E^*_t$ | 0.1316 (1.6301) | 0.1264 (1.5618) | 0.4797 (5.3007) | 0.2998 (2.7660) | 0.1446 (1.5830) | 0.1428 (1.7137) | | | | | | |
| $\Delta E^*_{t-1}$ | 0.1109 (2.3189) | 0.1080 (2.2550) | 0.2726 (4.7378) | 0.1718 (2.6059) | 0.1078 (1.9905) | 0.1150 (2.3270) | | | | | | |
| $\Delta E^*_{t-2}$ | 0.0820 (1.8134) | 0.0808 (1.7856) | 0.1236 (1.8952) | 0.0792 (1.2408) | 0.0714 (1.3938) | 0.0820 (1.7508) | | | | | | |
| $\Delta E^*_{t-3}$ | 0.0451 (1.3122) | 0.0448 (1.3040) | 0.0327 (0.6420) | 0.0219 (0.4532) | 0.0355 (0.9120) | 0.0436 (1.2272) | | | | | | |
| $\Delta P_t$ | 0.6703 (5.1587) | 0.6798 (5.2094) | | 0.4585 (2.7055) | 0.7236 (5.0197) | 0.6412 (4.7959) | 0.3907 (3.1103) | | | | | |
| $U^P_t$ | 0.2563 (2.6321) | 0.2960 (3.0538) | | | 0.4845 (5.5150) | 0.2813 (2.8128) | | | 0.0946 (0.6674) | 0.0716 (0.4976) | 0.0970 (0.6828) | 0.7775 (5.6638) |
| $G_t$ | 0.2214 (3.9106) | 0.2150 (3.8393) | | | | 0.1933 (3.3930) | | 0.3316 (4.8966) | 0.2982 (3.5336) | 0.3191 (3.6523) | 0.3140 (3.6312) | |
| $(T/E^*)_{t-1}$ | −0.0593 (−2.1429) | | | | | | | | | −0.0408 (−0.9384) | | |
| $(T/E^*)^{-1}_{t-1}$ | | 67.7200 (2.1384) | | | | | | | | | 43.4826 (0.8763) | |

NOTE: Figures in parentheses are estimated '$t$' values.

that each individual coefficient of $\Delta E^*_{t-i}$ is significantly different from zero except that of $\Delta E^*_{t-3}$, and the $F$ statistic shows that the overall relationship is significant. The next most dominant variable is $G$ (Regression 8) with a $\bar{R}^2$ of 29 per cent and a significant positive coefficient of $\hat{\beta} = 0.33$. All the other variables on their own explain at best 13 per cent of the variation in $\Delta T$.

The results in Table 3.3 indicate that the Ashenfelter and Pencavel model suffers from multicollinearity. When $G$ is the only explanatory variable (Regression 8) and $U^P$, $(T/E^*)_{t-1}$, and $(T/E^*)_{t-1}^{-1}$ are added (Regressions 9, 10, and 11), the $\bar{R}^2$ drops, implying that there is a degree of multicollinearity between these variables and $\Delta T$. The existence of multicollinearity is further confirmed by the fact that although the $F$ statistic indicates that the coefficients of all these variables are significantly different from zero when considered simultaneously, they are not, with the exception of $G$, significantly different from zero when examined individually by means of a '$t$' test.[54] Similarly, when the $\Delta E^*$ terms are the only regressors (Regression 3) and $\Delta P$, $U^P$, and $G$ are introduced (Regressions 4, 5, and 6), the coefficients of $\Delta E^*$ are reduced.[55] In fact, they are almost halved when $\Delta P$ is introduced, almost halved again when $U^P$ is introduced, and remain stable when $G$ is introduced. The existence of multicollinearity does not bias the estimates, but it does make them imprecise. And this imprecision means, in particular, that no firm conclusions can be drawn about the size of the impact of $\Delta E^*$ upon $\Delta T$.[56]

A related problem concerns the variable $G$. It fluctuates within a relatively small range: minimum, 30 per cent; mean, 53 per cent; and maximum, 78 per cent. As a result of $G$'s lack of variability, it interacts with the constant term. As can be seen from Regressions 3, 4, and 12, the constant term has a positive sign, a reasonable magnitude, and is significantly different from zero when $G$ is excluded. But when $G$ is the only regressor (as in Regression 8), or when G is included with other variables, the constant term remains significant but becomes extremely

54. These two techniques for detecting multicollinearity are discussed by J. Kmenta, *Elements of Econometrics* (London: Macmillan, 1971), 389–90. See also Appendix A below for a discussion of multicollinearity.
55. It may be that the original coefficients of $\Delta E^*$ in Regression 3 are high as a result of omitting other relevant explanatory variables which are correlated with the $\Delta E^*$ regressors. But, whichever way it is viewed, multicollinearity definitely exists.
56. The imprecision arises because of the large variances of the least squares estimators. For example, the estimated impact of the $\Delta E^*$ terms in the first regression of Table 3.2 should not be interpreted as 0.367 but as a point lying anywhere between 0 and 0.78 at the 95 per cent confidence level. See above, p. 38, n. 40, for the implications which Ashenfelter and Pencavel draw from the estimated size of the $\Delta E^*$ coefficients.

large and negative.[57] This sensitivity of the constant term to the introduction of $G$ should not be ignored. In fact, it justifies Mancke's point that the coefficient of $G$ exaggerates the true effect of a change in $G$ on $\Delta T$.[58]

Finally, there is a problem with Ashenfelter and Pencavel's sub-period analysis. They claim that 'there is no consistent evidence in favor of amending the analysis to make special cases' of the four sub-periods which they examine. They suggest that the large negative residual for 1919 is accounted for by an anomaly in the data used to construct $U^P$ while the large positive residual for 1936 is explained by the 'stimulating effect of the National Labor Relations Act passed the previous year'.[59] Leaving aside the fact that, given Ashenfelter and Pencavel's argument, $G$ might reasonably be expected to take care of the effect of the Wagner Act, it is clear from Figure 3.1 that there are higher positive and negative residuals than the two mentioned. But since they lie outside the sub-periods specified, no attempt is made to explain them. There is clearly a need for a more broadly based sub-period analysis.

The above criticism is not meant to detract from the fundamental importance of Ashenfelter and Pencavel's work: it represents a pioneering and innovative attempt to assess quantitatively the determinants of union growth. Although it contains various weaknesses, it has reinvigorated the discussion of union growth and pointed the way forward for future work in this area. Indeed, not the least of its significance is that it has encouraged Sharpe to develop a similar model for Australia.

## The Sharpe Model

Sharpe's model, a lineal descendant of that of Ashenfelter and Pencavel, attempts to explain Australian union growth between 1907 and 1969 in predominantly economic terms.[60] His basic equation is

$$\Delta T_t = a_0 + a_1 (T/E^*)_{t-1} + a_2 \Delta E_t^* + a_3 U_t + a_4 C_t$$
$$+ \sum_{i=0}^{X} a_{5+i} \Delta(W/P)_{t-i} + \epsilon_t$$

where $\epsilon$ is a random disturbance term, and the expected signs are

57. When $U^P$ is the only regressor, the constant term also becomes negative. But its magnitude is small, and it is not significantly different from zero.
58. *op. cit.*, 190, n. 9.
59. Ashenfelter and Pencavel (1969), *op. cit.*, 445, n. 1.
60. *op. cit.*

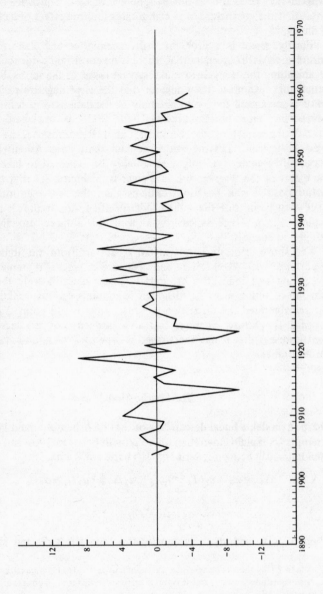

FIGURE 3.1

ESTIMATED RESIDUALS GENERATED BY THE
ASHENFELTER AND PENCAVEL MODEL

positive for $a_2$ and $a_4$ and negative for $a_1$, $a_3$, and $a_5$. The nature of the explanatory variables is discussed in turn below.

$(T/E^*)$ is the ratio of total trade union membership to employment in the 'unionized' sectors.[61] Although Sharpe specifies this variable in a similar fashion to Ashenfelter and Pencavel, he justifies it in a slightly different way. He follows Berkowitz[62] in viewing a union as a business organization whose role is to provide services such as collective bargaining, education, and political action. In providing these services, a union incurs expenditures which it attempts to cover by selling membership subscriptions. Like any typical business firm, a union must equate expenditures and revenues if it is to survive. On the basis of this logic, Sharpe claims that a recruitment drive by a union usually involves expenditure of part of its capital funds, and hence the size of these funds determines the amount of recruiting it attempts to undertake. Appropriate data on union capital funds for testing this hypothesis do not exist. So Sharpe reformulates the hypothesis and argues that

for any fixed level of capital funds, the ability of the union to attract new membership depends on the per capita organizational cost. When per capita organizational costs are high the drain on union capital funds will be greater, forcing unions to curtail some of their organizing activities. Alternatively, as the proportion of wage and salary earners unionized increases, unions must begin tapping workers who are not as susceptible to the 'organization virus' and hence their organization and subsequent servicing will be more costly. Thus, all other things remaining unaltered, the higher the proportion of workers already unionized, the lower we would predict the growth rate of union membership to be.[63]

In short, Sharpe claims that the *per capita* organizing costs determine the amount of recruiting activity unions can initiate, and he puts $(T/E^*)$ forward as a proxy for the level of these costs in a given year.

$\Delta E^*$ is the rate of change of employment (excluding unemployment) in the 'unionized' sectors of the economy, and Sharpe's grounds for including it in his model are similar to those of Ashenfelter and Pencavel. He claims that union organizing drives are more likely to be successful in periods of increasing employment. In addition, he suggests

---

61. The 'unionized' sectors are defined as mining and quarrying; manufacturing; gas, electricity, and water supply; building and construction; transport and communication; and public administration.
62. Monroe Berkowitz, 'The Economics of Trade Union Organization and Administration', *Industrial and Labor Relations Review*, VII (July 1954), 575–92.
63. *op. cit.*, 139.

that increasing employment is likely to lead, via union security provisions, to automatic increases in union membership.[64]

$U$ is the level of unemployment. Sharpe offers two reasons for suggesting that it is negatively related to union growth. First, 'the large pool of unemployed workers represents a threat to the standards of living of those at work.' Second, 'union dues become more of a burden to the member, tending to increase the relative cost of membership.'[65]

$\Delta(W/P)$ is the annual percentage rate of change of real wage rates. Sharpe suggests that it is negatively related to union growth because 'as real wages decline, workers' discontent usually increases so that their desire to organize in order to retain their real wage is highest.'[66] On the assumption that workers only slowly adjust their behaviour in response to changes in real wages, he specifies $\Delta(W/P)$ in distributed lag form.[67] He finds from experimenting with the data that a two-year lag is the most appropriate.

$C$ is a dummy variable which is introduced into the model to capture the impact of compulsory arbitration legislation in Australia upon union growth during the early years of the twentieth century.[68] This legislation enabled workers to take an employer before a court or tribunal, and thereby often obtain better wages and working conditions than they otherwise would have enjoyed. But workers could appear before these bodies and receive awards only if they were represented by a registered union, and this encouraged many of them to become union members. Sharpe experiments with two types of dummy variables. The first, $C\lambda$, is based on the assumption that the legislation factor exerts a positive impact on union growth but that it 'decays' over time in a geometric manner.[69] But Sharpe finds that $C\lambda$ is highly correlated with $T/E^*$ and that when the two variables are used jointly as regressors, the coefficient of $C\lambda$ is 'negative and highly insignificant'.[70] Hence he formulates a second dummy variable, $C2$, which is defined to equal the

---

64. *ibid.*, 140. Sharpe also tried lagged values of $\Delta E^*$ but found that their coefficients 'were of the wrong sign and highly insignificant'. See *ibid.*, 144.
65. *ibid.*, 140.
66. *ibid.*
67. In other words, he assumes that union growth depends upon a short moving average of previous rates of change in real wages.
68. Before including this variable in the model, Sharpe attempted to use a political variable similar to that employed by Ashenfelter and Pencavel. He used the proportion of the electorate who voted for the Australian Labor Party in the House of Representatives, but found that its coefficient was 'highly insignificant'. See *ibid.*, 141.
69. That is, $C\lambda_t = (\lambda)^r$ where $r = (t - 1907)$ and $0 < \lambda < 1$. $\lambda$ is selected so that the $R^2$ of the regression equation is maximized.
70. He suggests that this result is caused by the multicollinearity problem. See *ibid.*, 142.

value of unity from 1907 to 1913 and zero thereafter on the assumption that union growth during this period is higher by a fixed constant as a result of the favourable impact of compulsory arbitration.

Sharpe estimates the above equation by means of the ordinary least squares technique. The results are given in Table 3.4. He finds, as Regression 1 indicates, that the coefficients of all the explanatory variables possess the expected signs, that their '$t$' values are all significantly different from zero at the 5 per cent level, and that the

TABLE 3.4

## SHARPE'S DETERMINANTS OF THE RATE OF CHANGE OF UNION MEMBERSHIP IN AUSTRALIA, 1907–1969

| REGRESSION | 1 | 2 | 3 | 4 | 5 |
|---|---|---|---|---|---|
| Summary Statistics | | | | | |
| $\bar{R}^2$ | 0.758 | 0.753 | 0.746 | 0.726 | 0.699 |
| SEE | 2.84 | 2.87 | 2.91 | 3.02 | 3.17 |
| DW | 1.86 | 1.86 | 1.91 | 1.66 | 1.64 |
| Estimated Coefficients | | | | | |
| Constant | 14.18 | 14.25 | 15.44 | 5.13 | 4.03 |
| | (4.39) | (4.35) | (3.24) | (6.88) | (4.75) |
| $(T/E^*)_{t-1}$ | −11.88 | −12.03 | −14.19 | | |
| | (−2.87) | (−2.85) | (−3.50) | | |
| $\Delta E_t^*$ | 0.48 | 0.48 | 0.45 | 0.49 | 0.62 |
| | (5.10) | (5.00) | (4.76) | (4.90) | (6.21) |
| $U_t$ | −0.36 | −0.36 | −0.31 | −0.41 | −0.44 |
| | (−3.94) | (−3.84) | (−3.48) | (−4.39) | (−4.45) |
| $(C2)_t$ | 4.54 | 4.51 | 3.98 | 9.63 | |
| | (2.09) | (2.20) | (1.80) | (7.20) | |
| $(C\lambda)_t$ | | | | | 11.53 |
| | | | | | (6.48) |
| $\Delta(W/P)_t$ | −0.21 | −0.22 | | −0.31 | −0.26 |
| | (−1.91) | (−1.90) | | (−2.70) | (−2.12) |
| $\Delta(W/P)_{t-1}$ | −0.22 | −0.21 | −0.23 | −0.27 | −0.28 |
| | (−2.14) | (−1.86) | (−2.14) | (−2.49) | (−2.45) |
| $\Delta(W/P)_{t-2}$ | −0.25 | −0.25 | −0.16 | −0.36 | −0.29 |
| | (−2.10) | (−2.09) | (−1.42) | (−3.00) | (−2.28) |
| $\Delta(W/P)_{t-3}$ | | 0.03 | | | |
| | | (0.23) | | | |

NOTE: Figures in parentheses are the estimated '$t$' values of the regression coefficients.

Durbin–Watson statistic does not indicate the presence of autocorrelated residuals.[71] A comparison of Regressions 4 and 5, in which $T/E^*$ has been omitted because of the multicollinearity problem referred to above, reveals that 'the arbitrarily specified dummy variable, $C2$, produces a higher $\bar{R}^2$ value than $C\lambda$, the dummy which does have some *a priori* justification.' Since $\Delta T$ and $\Delta(W/P)_t$ in Regression 1 may be mutually dependent, Regression 3 omits $\Delta(W/P)_t$ and avoids any simultaneity problem which may exist, by including only predetermined changes in real wages. Although this results in the coefficient of $\Delta(W/P)_{t-2}$ no longer being significantly different from zero at the 5 per cent level, Sharpe concludes that 'it is evident that none of the major conclusions of this study are altered in moving from Regression 1 to Regression 3.' Finally, Sharpe compares the actual and predicted values of trade union growth in eight sub-periods, and concludes that 'with the possible exceptions of 1907–1910 and 1941–1945 it is evident that the model formulated in this study provides an adequate explanation of Australian trade union membership growth.'[72]

Sharpe's results are not as impressive as they might at first appear. To begin with, the theoretical justification and specification of some of the explanatory variables is questionable. $\Delta E^*$ has the drawback, as the above discussion of Ashenfelter and Pencavel's work indicated, of mixing together three separate employment effects and thereby making it impossible to distinguish empirically between them.[73] And, as Mancke pointed out in the case of the Ashenfelter and Pencavel model, there are *a priori* reasons for doubting that the relationship between $\Delta T$ and $T/E^*$ has always been linear and negative as Sharpe suggests.[74] In addition, given that $T/E^*$ is supposed to be a measure of the difficulty and hence the cost of recruiting the unorganized, it would seem to make more sense to use total union potential in the denominator rather than merely employment in the unionized sectors.[75] In any case, it is debatable to what extent the size of a union's capital funds determines the amount of recruiting it is able or willing to undertake. For

---

71. Sharpe notes that the inclusion of a form of the lagged dependent variable, $(T/E^*)_{t-1}$, biases the DW statistic towards this conclusion. But he points out that Regression 4, which excludes $(T/E^*)_{t-1}$, also shows little evidence of autocorrelation.
72. *ibid.*, 145. The eight sub-periods are 1907–13, 1914–18, 1919–27, 1928–33, 1934–40, 1941–5, 1946–54, and 1955–69.
73. See above, pp. 38–9.
74. See above, p. 40.
75. The two series differ quite considerably. Sharpe himself points out that whereas the 'true' density series reaches its peak in 1954, $T/E^*$ reaches its peak in 1932 as a result of $E^*$ declining very much more than $T$ during the early years of the depression. See *op. cit.*, 152.

recruiting is not necessarily undertaken by full-time officials launching systematic and expensive organizing campaigns, but is often accomplished by existing members and shop stewards at relatively little cost to the union. Finally, although $C2$ is formulated on the assumption that trade union growth between 1907 and 1913 is higher by a fixed constant as a result of the impact of compulsory arbitration, Sharpe himself points out that strictly speaking 'the dummy variable cannot be associated with the effect of compulsory arbitration any more than with anything else.'[76]

Regardless of the adequacy of the theoretical justification and specification of the various variables, the way in which some of them are quantified is unsatisfactory. In calculating real wage rates, Sharpe uses a different long-run price series from that offered by the Commonwealth Statistician, and he offers no reason for doing so.[77] Moreover, his wage series only covers manual males for the period 1907—52, but includes both males and females for the period 1953—69. It is not altogether clear how Sharpe derived a total manual male and female wage series since such a series has not been constructed by the Commonwealth Statistician. In any case, since female wages are not available for the earlier period, it would have been more consistent to ignore them in the later period and simply use male wages throughout. Finally, since the Commonwealth Statistician did not publish an employment series until after the Second World War, Sharpe had to piece his $\Delta E^*$ together from a variety of sources using a variety of estimating methods. As he himself points out, the resulting series, particularly for the years 1907—11, could contain 'substantial errors'.[78] Measurement errors in the explanatory variables will obviously render his estimates biased and inconsistent.

Even if Sharpe's analysis were free of these statistical difficulties, it would still be characterized by serious methodological shortcomings. These can most easily be demonstrated by re-running his model using different combinations of the explanatory variables and analysing the contribution which each of these makes. The results are given in Table 3.5.

76. *op. cit.*, 153, n. 14.
77. Sharpe uses the 'A' series regimen for 1907 to 1929; the 'C' series regimen for 1930 to 1953; and the Consumer Price Index for 1954 to 1969. The Commonwealth Statistician uses the 'A' series regimen from 1907 to 1914; the 'C' series regimen from 1914 to 1946—7; a composite of the CPI Housing Group and the 'C' series index from 1946—7 to 1948—9; and the CPI from 1948—9 onwards. Compare Sharpe, *op. cit.*, 152 with *Labour Report*, no. 56 (Canberra: Commonwealth Bureau of Census and Statistics, 1971), 41.
78. *op. cit.*, 151.

TABLE
A RE-RUN OF THE SHARPE MODEL OF

| REGRESSION | 1 | 2 | 3 | 4 | 5 | 6 | 7 |
|---|---|---|---|---|---|---|---|
| **Summary Statistics** | | | | | | | |
| $R^2$ | 0.8153 | 0.8041 | 0.8110 | 0.7738 | 0.7656 | 0.5892 | 0.2621 |
| $\bar{R}^2$ | 0.7874 | 0.7695 | 0.7865 | 0.7444 | 0.7352 | 0.5757 | 0.2379 |
| SEE | 2.3930 | 2.4320 | 2.3950 | 2.6200 | 2.6670 | 3.7320 | 4.9999 |
| F | 33.4143 | 26.1665 | 38.6279 | 30.7792 | 29.4009 | 87.4877 | 21.6697 |
| df | 7, 53 | 8, 51 | 6, 54 | 6, 54 | 6, 54 | 1, 61 | 1, 61 |
| DW | 1.4730 | 1.3841 | 1.4676 | 1.3030 | 1.2426 | 1.2707 | 0.7225 |
| **Estimated Coefficients** | | | | | | | |
| Constant | 14.1793 (5.1127) | 14.2643 (4.9580) | 14.7983 (5.4381) | 4.8298 (7.4178) | 3.6339 (4.9536) | 23.6334 (11.1379) | 2.5150 (3.4209) |
| $(T/E^*)_{t-1}$ | −12.2928 (−3.4512) | −12.3571 (−3.3167) | −13.4337 (−3.9339) | | | −25.4244 (−9.3535) | |
| $\Delta E^*_t$ | 0.5554 (6.8620) | 0.5530 (6.5468) | 0.5462 (6.7709) | 0.5673 (6.3978) | 0.6861 (8.0361) | | 0.7026 (4.6551) |
| $U_t$ | −0.3427 (−4.4659) | −0.3435 (−4.3493) | −0.3196 (−4.3211) | −0.4019 (−4.9000) | −0.4169 (−5.0092) | | |
| $(C2)_t$ | 3.5927 (1.9273) | 3.7426 (1.9307) | 3.2891 (1.7805) | 8.4391 (6.2788) | | | |
| $\Delta(W/P)_t$ | −0.1067 (−1.1018) | −0.0949 (−0.9261) | | −0.2039 (−2.0067) | −0.1365 (−1.2959) | | |
| $\Delta(W/P)_{t-1}$ | −0.2928 (−3.2349) | −0.3088 (−3.0201) | −0.2981 (−3.2916) | −0.3511 (−3.6012) | −0.3524 (−3.5484) | | |
| $\Delta(W/P)_{t-2}$ | −0.2179 (−2.1954) | −0.2073 (−1.9783) | −0.1733 (−1.9085) | −0.3283 (−3.1863) | −0.2558 (−2.3896) | | |
| $\Delta(W/P)_{t-3}$ | | −0.0270 (−0.2738) | | | | | |
| $(C\lambda)_t$ | | | | | 11.1918 (6.0155) | | |

NOTE: Figures in parentheses are estimated '$t$' values.

The first and most important problem, as can be seen by comparing Regressions 1 to 5 in Table 3.5 with those in Table 3.4, is that it proved impossible to duplicate Sharpe's model. The Durbin–Watson statistic provides the most serious discrepancy between the two sets of results. Sharpe's published Durbin–Watson statistics do not indicate the presence of autocorrelated residuals, but the results in Table 3.5 suggest that there is evidence of positive autocorrelation.[79] Its presence invalidates the significance tests and also implies that the model is misspecified, or that the dependent variable $(\Delta T)$ contains relatively large measurement errors,[80] or that both factors occur. In short, it casts considerable doubt upon Sharpe's conclusions.

79. See Appendix A for a discussion of autocorrelation and the Durbin–Watson statistic.
80. The Australian union membership series, like all union membership series, contains measurement errors, particularly for the years before 1912. Sharpe

3.5
AUSTRALIAN UNION GROWTH, 1907–1969

| 8 | 9 | 10 | 11 | 12 | 13 | 14 | 15 |
|---|---|---|---|---|---|---|---|
| 0.1018 | 0.0757 | 0.6992 | 0.3273 | 0.6283 | 0.6171 | 0.7076 | 0.6662 |
| 0.0723 | 0.0109 | 0.6842 | 0.2937 | 0.6098 | 0.5979 | 0.6877 | 0.6435 |
| 5.5165 | 5.1555 | 3.2190 | 4.8136 | 3.5780 | 3.6320 | 3.2000 | 3.4190 |
| 6.9099 | 1.5566 | 69.7413 | 14.5963 | 50.7180 | 48.3452 | 47.5842 | 39.2427 |
| 1, 61 | 3, 57 | 2, 60 | 2, 60 | 2, 60 | 2, 60 | 3, 59 | 3, 59 |
| 0.6209 | 0.5807 | 1.5296 | 0.7570 | 1.3275 | 1.3228 | 1.5546 | 1.4731 |
| | | | | | | | |
| 6.2840 | 4.5843 | 20.3085 | 4.2467 | 39.0924 | 16.6137 | 16.5803 | 17.1781 |
| (6.0904) | (5.7554) | (10.3433) | (4.2114) | (6.0350) | (4.2140) | (4.7720) | (4.6212) |
| | | −22.6070 | | −42.9451 | −17.0115 | −18.0608 | −15.9194 |
| | | (−9.3377) | | (−5.7712) | (−3.5319) | (−4.2478) | (−3.4985) |
| | | 0.4699 | 0.6572 | | | 0.4386 | |
| | | (4.6850) | (4.4852) | | | (4.2726) | |
| −0.4291 | | | −0.3463 | | | | −0.3006 |
| (−2.6287) | | | (−2.4110) | | | | (−2.9450) |
| | | | | | 5.5398 | 3.1176 | 5.6168 |
| | | | | | (2.0904) | (1.2972) | (2.2507) |
| | −0.0775 | | | | | | |
| | (−0.4005) | | | | | | |
| | −0.3479 | | | | | | |
| | (−1.8711) | | | | | | |
| | −0.1409 | | | | | | |
| | (−0.7210) | | | | | | |
| | | | | −13.3835 | | | |
| | | | | (−2.5138) | | | |

Even taking his results at their face value, his work still presents certain methodological difficulties. It can be seen from Table 3.5 that 58 per cent of the variation in $\Delta T$ is explained by $T/E^*$ alone (Regression 6) and that 68 per cent is explained by $T/E^*$ and $\Delta E^*$ jointly (Regression 10).[81] $U$, the $\Delta(W/P)$ terms, and $C$ add relatively

---

is aware of these errors and there is little that he or anyone else can do to eliminate them. See Bain and Price, *op. cit.*

81. Statistically speaking, this result is not surprising. $T/E^*$ exhibits very little variation and hence is a classic example of a variable whose estimated coefficient is highly correlated with the estimated coefficient of the constant. Indeed, the correlation between the two regression coefficients is −0.98. It can also be seen, by comparing Regressions 4 and 5 with Regressions 1, 2 and 3, that the magnitude and sign of the constant term is very sensitive to the introduction of $T/E^*$. This point has already been discussed in relation to Ashenfelter and Pencavel's work (above, pp. 44–5).

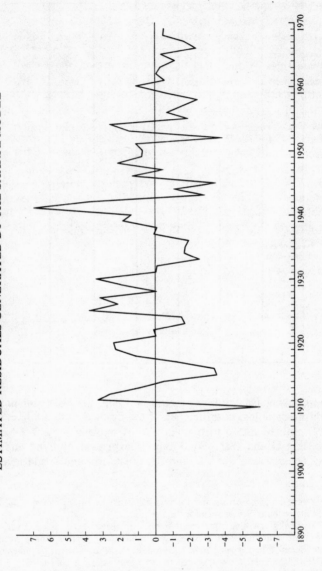

FIGURE 3.2
ESTIMATED RESIDUALS GENERATED BY THE SHARPE MODEL

little. In other words, the explanatory power of Sharpe's model depends primarily upon $T/E^*$ and $\Delta E^*$, the two variables which are most suspect on theoretical grounds.[82]

Finally, as can be seen from Figure 3.2, the residuals obtained from Sharpe's regressions are clustered.[83] This implies that relevant explanatory variables have been omitted and that the regression coefficients are biased. Sharpe should have examined these clusters and tried to eliminate them by including the relevant omitted variables.[84] At the very least, he should have tried to minimize the effects of these clusters by introducing dummy variables corresponding to each cluster. This assumes, of course, that he could offer a rationale for these dummies. As his analysis stands at the moment, Sharpe has simply offered certain *ad hoc* and, in some cases, inadequate reasons for the discrepancy between his predicted values of $\Delta T$ and its actual values in the various sub-periods.[85]

Sharpe's work represents primarily an attempt to apply an Ashenfelter–Pencavel type of model to Australian data. He suggests a few interesting modifications to the model: the use of $U$ to measure more directly the impact of the excess demand for labour and the use of $\Delta(W/P)$ to measure more directly the effect of real wages. But the theoretical, statistical, and methodological weaknesses which characterize his work clearly limit the significance which can be attached to his specific findings.

## Conclusion

This chapter has described and evaluated three econometric models which have been advanced by Hines, Ashenfelter and Pencavel, and Sharpe to explain trade union growth in Britain, the United States, and Australia. All the models rely primarily upon economic variables. But

82. See the discussion of these variables, above, pp. 50–51.
83. All his regressions generate clustered residuals. An obvious example is the negative cluster of residuals for the period 1955–69.
84. Sharpe tried to eliminate the negative residual cluster for 1955–69 by introducing the proportion of women in the labour force as an explanatory variable. But he found that its coefficient was insignificant.
85. For example, he tries to explain away the tendency of his model to overestimate during the period 1914–18 by suggesting that the unemployment rate is understated because 'for many adventurous and patriotic workers, unemployment was often an occasion for enlistment' (*op. cit.*, 147). Yet the average unemployment rate of 3.9 per cent for the five-year period 1914–18 is greater than the average unemployment rate of 3.3 per cent for the immediately preceding five-year period 1909–13.

those of Sharpe and, in particular, Ashenfelter and Pencavel also contain social and political variables.

The results produced by these models can easily be summarized. All of them suggest that real wages are an important determinant of union growth regardless of whether their effect is measured explicitly as the rate of change of real wages or implicitly as the rate of change of retail prices. Another variable which emerges as significant in all the models is some measure of the extent to which the labour force is already unionized. But the exact definition of this variable, the specific form of its relationship to union growth, and its theoretical justification vary among the models. The profits variable, as a proxy for the general prosperity of industry, produces less clear-cut results. Although it is generally significant in Hines's model, its sign is highly variable and its effect is very small. And when the profit rate and the rate of change of money profits were added successively to Ashenfelter and Pencavel's model, neither of them were found to be significant.

All of the models include measures of employment and unemployment in order to pick up the effect of labour market 'tightness'. In his preliminary analysis, Hines uses both the level and the rate of change of unemployment as well as other measures of excess demand for labour, but finds that none of them makes a significant contribution to the explanation of union growth. In contrast, Sharpe finds that the level of unemployment is a significant determinant of union growth in Australia. Sharpe also uses the rate of change of employment in the unionized sectors of the economy, as do Ashenfelter and Pencavel, and both studies find that this variable is highly significant.

Ashenfelter and Pencavel and Sharpe also introduce non-economic variables into their models. Ashenfelter and Pencavel use peak unemployment as a measure of the 'stock of grievances' which cause workers to be discontented and to join unions as a form of protest. They also use the percentage of Democrats in the United States House of Representatives as a proxy for public opinion and labour legislation. The effect of labour legislation is represented in Sharpe's model by a dummy variable. All these variables are found to be important determinants of union growth, but since they all pose problems of interpretation it is difficult to know what significance to attach to this finding.

These three models indicate that it is possible to apply econometric methods to the study of union growth. More important, they also demonstrate the utility of doing so: the theoretical notions which exist can be tested more precisely, and firmer conclusions can be drawn about the relative importance of the various explanatory variables. Nevertheless, all the models discussed in this chapter possess

56

## Conclusion

theoretical, methodological, and statistical weaknesses which limit the confidence which can be placed in the results they produce. In an attempt to remove these deficiencies, the following chapter uses the conclusions which emerge from the work of Hines, Ashenfelter and Pencavel, and Sharpe to build an alternative model of union growth.

# 4

# An Alternative Model of Union Growth

This chapter attempts to build a model of union growth which is free of various weaknesses possessed by previous models. It begins by examining the problems involved in specifying the dependent variable. It then discusses the nature of the explanatory variables and the rationale for including them in the model. It continues by raising some questions concerning the nature of the functional forms and the lag structures by which the two sets of variables are linked. And it concludes by estimating the model on the basis of the data which are available for the United Kingdom.

## The Specification of the Model

### The Dependent Variable
The first problem in specifying the dependent variable is to decide whether to work with actual union membership or the density of union membership as given by the formula

$$\frac{\text{Actual Union Membership}}{\text{Potential Union Membership}} \times 100.$$

The simpler and more direct procedure is to use union density. Taking potential union membership into account enables one of the most obvious determinants of union growth to be held constant and hence controlled for in the subsequent inquiry into causation. This is particularly advantageous in cross-section studies where comparisons are being made at a single point in time across different industries, occupations, firms, or geographical regions with widely varying potential union memberships.

But in longitudinal studies where year-to-year changes in potential union membership are generally quite small, there are reasons for preferring actual union membership as the dependent variable. To begin with, the use of union density as the dependent variable constrains the relationship between actual and potential union membership to be strictly proportional. But there is no tautological reason, as Ashenfelter and Pencavel have pointed out, why a given change in potential union membership should automatically produce the same proportionate change in actual union membership.[1] Given a lack of proportionality, the impact of potential union membership upon union growth must be allowed for on the right-hand side of the equation. This can be accomplished by using union density as an explanatory variable. There are also other reasons, as previous work in this area as well as the next section of this chapter demonstrate, why the union density variable must be used on the right-hand side of the equation.[2] But there is no reason why it should be used on the left-hand side of the equation, and such a use could give rise to statistical problems. For the potential membership component of union density is generally characterized by considerable measurement error,[3] and it is well known that such error in the dependent variable tends to produce autocorrelation.[4] Moreover, to use union density on the left-hand side of the equation would increase the possibility of spurious correlation.[5] Hence for all these

---

1. 'American Trade Union Growth: 1900–1960', *Quarterly Journal of Economics*, LXXXIII (August 1969), 444, n. 6.
2. See above, Chapter 3, and below, pp. 67–8.
3. For not only are there considerable conceptual difficulties involved in defining exactly who is a potential union member, but there are also immense practical problems in obtaining accurate and internally consistent data on potential union membership over time. See G. S. Bain and R. J. Price, *Profiles of Union Growth* (Oxford: Blackwell, forthcoming) for a discussion of the conceptual and empirical problems involved in computing potential union membership. Perhaps the major difficulty is that historical series of potential union membership have to be pieced together from a variety of sources, including interpolations of decennial census of population data.
4. See Appendix A as well as J. Kmenta, *Elements of Econometrics* (London: Macmillan, 1971), 269–96 and A. Koutsoyiannis, *Theory of Econometrics* (London: Macmillan, 1973), 194–222, for a discussion of this problem.
5. The following model makes use of unemployment as an explanatory variable. Unemployment is related to potential union membership $(L^*)$ through the identity $U^* + E^* \equiv L^*$, where $U^*$ is unemployment, $E^*$ is employment, and $L^*$ is the labour force, in all cases excluding employers, the self-employed, and the armed forces. Hence if union density $(T/L^*)$ were used as the dependent variable, there would be a spurious negative correlation between $T/L^*$ and $U$. There would also be a spurious correlation between the dependent variable and the explanatory variable, $(T/L^*)_{t-1}$.

reasons it seems best to use actual union membership rather than the density of union membership as the dependent variable.[6]

Given that union membership is the appropriate dependent variable, the next problem is to decide whether to specify it as a level or as a rate of change. In one sense it does not matter, for there is no formal difficulty in transforming the one into the other.[7] But since the subject of union *growth* is by its very nature more concerned with rates of change than with levels, the more direct approach is to formulate the dependent variable in a dynamic way. Even if this were not so, there are compelling methodological reasons for preferring a rate of change formulation. Variables specified in terms of levels are much more likely to be characterized by time trends, and these greatly increase the likelihood of spurious correlation,[8] autocorrelation,[9] and multi-collinearity.[10] Even if the variables are not dominated by time trends, a level model runs a greater risk of being bedevilled by multicollinearity. For it generally requires a greater number of independent variables than a rate of change model to achieve the same degree of explanatory power; and the greater the number of independent variables the greater the likelihood of multicollinearity.[11]

The final problem in specifying the dependent variable is to decide

6. Both union membership and the density of union membership were used in the preliminary empirical work which was undertaken on British data. Although the results were broadly similar, union membership was preferred for the reasons given above.
7. The transformation becomes more difficult, however, if a model in which the dependent variable is specified as a level contains explanatory variables which have to be specified as rates of change.
8. The correlation between the variables is spurious if it results not from their intrinsic qualities but from their time trends; these time trends represent, in effect, other variables which are generally omitted from the equation.
9. See Appendix A and Kmenta, *loc. cit.*, for a discussion of this problem.
10. The existence of time trends in the dependent variable may produce a tendency for it to increase even if there is no change in the explanatory variables. In a rate of change equation, such a tendency is accounted for by the constant term. In a level equation, it can only be accounted for by adding a time trend variable, and this seriously increases the degree of multi-collinearity. See *ibid.*, 380–91. The general problem of multicollinearity is discussed below in Appendix A.
11. The alternative is to reduce the number of explanatory variables by adopting a restrictive lag structure. This procedure has two disadvantages. First, the lag structure must apply to all the variables in the regression equation at least after a certain point. Second, it necessitates the use of the lagged dependent variable as an explanatory variable; this yields biased estimates and, if autocorrelation is present, the regression coefficients will also be inconsistent. The Almon lag structure does not suffer from these disadvantages, but it has other serious handicaps. See J. Johnston, *Econometric Methods*, second edition (New York: McGraw-Hill, 1972), 294–8.

how to measure the rate of change. There are two basic options: an absolute rate of change or a proportional rate of change.[12] The latter is the more attractive option: the problem of measurement error in the union membership data is minimized,[13] and thinking in terms of percentage changes rather than in terms of absolute figures tied to specific levels is analytically easier and more interesting. Given that a proportional rate of change is preferable, the question arises whether it should be formulated in a discrete or a continuous fashion.[14] Since the one formulation is generally a fairly close approximation of the other, there is no overwhelming *a priori* argument for choosing between them. The choice must be made primarily on empirical grounds. Graphs indicated that the discrete and continuous formulations of the proportional rate of change of union membership are similar, and not surprisingly they produced similar results in the preliminary analysis of the data. Hence the remainder of this study cites only those results which relate to the discrete formulation of the proportional rate of change of union membership. In other words, the dependent variable of this study is $\Delta T_t = (T_t - T_{t-1})/T_t$.[15]

## The Explanatory Variables
The model's explanatory variables — prices, wages, unemployment, and union density — have all been mentioned by previous writers on union growth. But since these variables can and have been rationalized and specified in different and sometimes conflicting ways, it is worth discussing them further here in order to make clear exactly why they are included in the following model.

The Ashenfelter–Pencavel and Sharpe models of union growth have cast their explanatory variables largely within the framework of conventional economic analysis. They have tended to view unions as 'firms' and employees as 'customers' operating in a market where 'union services' are the commodity being sold and bought at a given price (membership subscription). The emphasis has tended to be on the demand side — the costs and benefits of union membership — but some attention has been given to the supply side, particularly by Sharpe in

---

12. An absolute rate of change is defined as $T_t - T_{t-1}$. A proportional rate of change is defined as $(T_t - T_{t-1})/T_t$, or as $(T_t - T_{t-1})/T_{t-1}$, or as a central difference such as $(T_{t+1} - T_{t-1})/2T_t$.
13. For a demonstration of this point see Ashenfelter and Pencavel, *op. cit.*, 440, n. 7.
14. Examples of a discrete proportional rate of change are given in n. 12. A continuous proportional rate of change is defined as $\log(T_t/T_{t-1})$.
15. All the explanatory variables which are specified as rates of change in the following model are formulated in the same way as the dependent variable; that is, as a discrete proportional rate of change.

his discussion of the determinants of union recruiting activity (selling costs).[16]

Useful as such an analytical framework may be, it has not been explicitly adopted here. For the objective of this study, of which this monograph forms only a part, is to integrate into a comprehensive theory the insights which several disciplines have to offer into the process of union growth. Hence the various explanatory variables are put forward here within the context of an analytical framework which is more methodologically neutral than that of supply and demand analyses and which is compatible not only with economics but also with the other disciplines upon which the wider study draws. More specifically, changes in union membership are seen as being determined by changes in both the *propensity* and the *opportunity* to unionize.[17] In other words, the following variables are held to have an impact upon union growth because they affect either the propensity to become or to cease to be a union member, the opportunity to become or to cease to be a union member, or both.

*Rate of change of retail prices* ($\Delta P$). Price rises may affect the propensity to unionize. For in as much as workers perceive an increase in the rate of change of retail prices as a threat to their standard of living – and there is a good deal of evidence which suggests that they generally do[18] – they are more likely to become and to remain union members in an attempt to maintain this standard. In addition, in so far as price rises are a proxy for the general prosperity of industry, they may also affect the opportunity to unionize. For employers may be more prepared to concede worker demands for better conditions and union recognition in periods of rising prices, partly because of a reluctance to have profitable production interrupted by industrial action and partly because increases in labour costs can be passed on

16. This framework is made even more explicit by Pencavel in 'The Demand for Union Services: An Exercise', *Industrial and Labor Relations Review*, XXIV (January 1971), 180–190. See also J. S. Lee, *An Economic Theory of Union Growth* (unpublished Ph.D thesis, University of Massachusetts, 1970).

17. This framework was suggested by some remarks of Lloyd Ulman in his discussion of Bernstein's work. See the *Proceedings of the Industrial Relations Research Association*, VII (December 1954), 237–8.

18. For example, Reynolds and Shister found in the United States that the most frequently cited factor in comments on the fairness of wages was the 'cost of maintaining an adequate standard of living'. See L. G. Reynolds and Joseph Shister, *Job Horizons* (New York: Harper, 1949), 23. Similarly, Behrend and her colleagues reported on the basis of an Irish survey that the most frequent specific reason given for the view that certain people were underpaid was the 'cost of living'. See H. Behrend *et al.*, *Views on Income Differentials and the Economic Situation* (Dublin: Economic and Social Research Institute, 1970), 29.

more easily to customers. In short, both the 'threat effect' and the 'prosperity effect' suggest that there will be a positive relationship between the rate of change of union membership and the rate of change of retail prices. But the positive impact of the latter upon the former will probably reflect the 'threat effect' more than the 'prosperity effect', for price rises and business prosperity do not always go together. To the extent that they do not, $\Delta P$ will not capture the 'prosperity effect'.[19]

*Rate of change of money wages* ($\Delta W$). Part of the above justification for the price variable implies that it is a proxy for real wages. And by using the price variable as a proxy in this way, it is possible to argue, as Ashenfelter and Pencavel have done, that the effect of real wages upon union growth can be tested without explicitly including a wage variable in the equation. But there are disadvantages in testing the argument in this implicit fashion. For price rises may not be a good proxy for real wages: prices may be increasing rapidly, but money wages may be increasing even more rapidly with the result that real wages are rising rather than falling. Moreover, regardless of what the relationship is between prices and money wages, if the latter is a relevant variable, as the above argument implies, then omitting it will result in the equation being misspecified and in the estimates of the various coefficients being biased and inconsistent.[20]

19. It might be argued that profits would make a better proxy than prices for the general prosperity of industry. But Hines's work (see above, pp. 26–33) suggests that the profits variable does not produce particularly good results. And Ashenfelter and Pencavel (*op. cit.*, 444, n. 4) found that neither the profit rate nor the rate of change of money profits was significantly related to union growth in the United States. In any case, the United Kingdom does not possess an internally consistent profit series covering the whole of the period 1893–1970.
20. The degree of bias depends upon the correlation between the explanatory variable which is included and that which is excluded as well as on the sign and magnitude of the parameter of the excluded variable in the true relation. Assume, in deviation form from sample means, that $Y_t = \beta_1 X_{1t} + \beta_2 X_{2t} + \epsilon_t$ is the true relationship, but that

$$Y_t = \beta_1 X_{1t} + \epsilon_t'$$

is estimated instead. Then it can be shown that

$$\text{plim}(\beta_1) = \beta_1 + \beta_2 \frac{\text{Cov}(X_1 X_2)}{\text{Var}(X_1)} .$$

Hence the bias will depend on

$$\beta_2 \text{ and } \frac{\text{Cov}(X_1 X_2)}{\text{Var}(X_1)}$$

or, in other words, on $\beta_2$ and the 'auxiliary' regression coefficient of $X_2$ on $X_1$.

Thus there are good methodological reasons for explicitly introducing a wage variable into the equation. There is also a good theoretical reason for doing so: wages may be important not only in relation to prices but also in their own right. For workers may unionize not only to defend an existing standard of living but also to improve that standard, and they may therefore expect unions to raise money wages regardless of what is happening to prices. Hence, when money wages are rising, workers may, rightly or wrongly, credit such rises to unions and hope that by beginning or continuing to support them they will do as well or even better in the future. In other words, it is possible that while a 'threat effect' may encourage workers to unionize when prices are rising, a 'credit effect' may lead them to unionize when money wages are rising. This possibility can only be allowed for by explicitly introducing a wage variable into the equation.

Granted that both $\Delta P$ and $\Delta W$ should be included in the equation, the question arises as to whether they should be introduced as two separate variables or, following Sharpe's example, as the ratio $\Delta(W/P)$. The answer to this question depends upon whether the impact of $\Delta P$ upon union growth is different in nature and magnitude from that of $\Delta W$. There are at least two reasons for expecting their impacts to be different. First, as the above discussion makes clear, the two variables may to some extent be capturing different effects. Hence, regardless of what is happening to $\Delta W$, if $\Delta P$ is increasing, unionization may increase as a result of the 'threat' and 'prosperity' effects. And regardless of what is happening to $\Delta P$, if $\Delta W$ is increasing, unionization may increase because of the 'credit effect'. Second, wages and prices will have a differential impact upon union growth if their saliency for workers is not the same. For example, if price rises are more salient than wage rises or if wage cuts are more salient than price cuts, then the magnitude of the coefficients of $\Delta P$ and $\Delta W$ will obviously be different.

Since there are good *a priori* reasons for expecting prices and wages to have a separate and distinct impact upon union growth, the procedure used in this and the following chapter is to begin by introducing $\Delta P$ and $\Delta W$ into the equation as two separate variables with positive signs expected for both of them for the reasons given above. While this approach enables conclusions to be drawn about the relative importance of the two variables and the various effects associated with them, it runs the risk of introducing multicollinearity into the equation as a result of the probable correlation between wages and prices. Even if it does this, however, such a procedure will still produce estimates which possess all the statistically desirable properties. Hence it is preferable to the approach which excludes the wage variable from the equation and thereby produces biased and inconsistent estimates.

If the multicollinearity problem is particularly serious, however, it will prove difficult to assess the separate effects of $\Delta P$ and $\Delta W$ upon union growth. In such circumstances, no information will be lost and the multicollinearity problem will be avoided if the combined effect of wages and prices is estimated by introducing them into the equation in the form of the ratio, $\Delta(W/P)$.[21] But since the use of $\Delta(W/P)$ constrains the effects of $\Delta P$ and $\Delta W$ to be equal in magnitude and opposite in sign, the validity of this constraint must be tested before the formulation can be used.[22] If the test indicates that the constraint is valid, then $\Delta(W/P)$ can be used in the equation instead of $\Delta W$ and $\Delta P$. And since the 'threat' and 'prosperity' effects suggest that $\Delta P$ must be positive, the expected sign for $\Delta(W/P)$ will be negative.[23]

If the test indicates that the constraint imposed by $\Delta(W/P)$ is not valid, then it cannot be introduced into the equation by itself.[24] But if the correlation between $\Delta P$ and $\Delta(W/P)$ is less than that between $\Delta P$ and $\Delta W$, then the former set of variables can be introduced into the equation in an attempt to overcome the multicollinearity problem and to loosen the restriction imposed by using $\Delta(W/P)$ on its own. In other words, allowing the coefficient of $\Delta P$ to be higher or lower in magnitude than that of $\Delta W$ allows for separate price and wage effects. And it is possible to predict a positive sign for $\Delta P$ on the grounds that it will primarily capture the 'threat' and 'prosperity' effects and a positive sign for $\Delta(W/P)$ on the grounds that it will primarily reflect the 'credit effect'.

*Level and/or rate of change of unemployment* $(U, \Delta U)$. Unemployment may affect the opportunity to unionize by influencing the relative bargaining power of employers and unions. When unemployment is high or increasing, employers may be better able and more willing to oppose unionism. For in so far as unemployment reduces the level of aggregate demand, production lost as a result of strikes and other forms of industrial action will be less costly to employers; indeed, such losses may even increase their profits. And if employers wish to maintain

21. The ratio $\Delta(W/P)$ is not the only form which could be used to overcome the multicollinearity problem. A difference form $(\Delta P - \Delta W)$ or any other weighted combination of the effects of the two variables could accomplish the same objective.
22. The test is described in Appendix B.3.
23. To show this, assume that $\Delta T = \alpha + \beta X + \gamma\Delta(W/P) + \epsilon$, where X is a vector of all other explanatory variables in the model. The partial effect of $\Delta P$ is equal to $-\gamma/(\Delta P)^2$. Hence if $\gamma$ is positive, then the effect of prices will be negative, and this is not acceptable given the above argument.
24. To introduce it would involve a specification error. For the test would be indicating that there is a difference in magnitude between the effects of $\Delta P$ and $\Delta W$, and to constrain them to be equal would be the same as omitting a relevant variable. In short, it would lead to biased and inconsistent estimates.

production in the face of industrial action, they can more easily do so by recruiting an alternative labour force from among the unemployed. Conversely, when unemployment is low or decreasing, the unions' strategical position tends to improve.

Unemployment may affect the propensity to become a union member in several ways. Unemployed workers may have little incentive to unionize because there is relatively little that a union can do for them. Moreover, the cost of union membership in dues and initiation fees is relatively greater for unemployed workers. Even if workers are not unemployed, they may be reluctant to join unions in periods of unemployment for fear of antagonizing their employers and thereby losing jobs which are in short supply.

Unemployment may also affect the propensity to remain a union member. The benefits which unions bring through collective bargaining have little relevance for unemployed members while the cost of membership is relatively greater for them. Moreover, in as much as unemployment reduces the ability of unions to win collective bargaining advances, the benefits of membership are reduced even for members who are not unemployed, and they may come to feel that union membership is no longer worthwhile.

But there are contrary forces at work, as Shister has pointed out, which may reduce the impact of unemployment upon the propensity to remain a union member.[25] Some unemployed workers have a financial incentive to try to maintain their union membership. For by doing so, they obtain unemployment benefit,[26] maintain their eligibility for other union 'friendly benefits' and perhaps even for company fringe benefits, receive information about job openings, and acquire access to those which exist in closed trades. Even if these economic reasons for retaining union membership do not exist, some unemployed members will be reluctant for social and political reasons to cut their links with the labour movement. And since many unions waive or at least reduce subscriptions for unemployed members, it often costs them little, if anything, to maintain their membership.

The above argument suggests that union growth and unemployment will be negatively related, but that the relationship is likely to be relatively weak and to be characterized by a lag. A lagged relationship is

---

25. Joseph Shister, 'The Logic of Union Growth', *Journal of Political Economy*, LXI (October 1953), 415–16; and *idem*, 'Unresolved Problems and New Paths for American Labor', *Industrial and Labor Relations Review*, IX (April 1956), 449–50.
26. Bakke has claimed that in Britain in the 1930s 'men tended to drop away from trade unions, when unemployed, unless their trade unions provided special services for the unemployed.' See E. Wight Bakke, *The Unemployed Man: A Social Study* (London: Nisbet, 1933), 17, 72, and 137.

also to be expected because most unions permit members to be in arrears for several months before dropping them from membership.[27] The estimated lag structure may indicate whether the level, the rate of change, or, indeed, both measures of unemployment should be included in the model.

*Level of union density* (D). The rate of change of union membership is also likely to be affected by the prevailing level of union density. Union density, as this chapter has already made clear, is given by the formula $T/L^* \times 100$, where $L^*$, or potential union membership, is defined to include all employees, whether employed or unemployed, who are legally permitted to unionize.[28] More specifically, potential union membership is the labour force minus employers, the self-employed, and, for all the countries included in this study except Sweden, members of the armed forces.

Since potential union membership is an inherent part of union density, including it on the right-hand side of the equation obviously helps to take into account the impact which potential union membership has upon union growth. But this is not the only reason for including union density as an explanatory variable.[29] A more important reason for including it is to capture the 'saturation effect': the greater difficulty of further increasing union membership as union density rises, partly because there are fewer workers left to recruit and partly because those who are left have less propensity and/or ability to unionize. As Rezler has pointed out,

It is obvious that as the . . . union movement embraces larger and larger portions of the organizable segment it gets nearer and nearer to the saturation point when each per cent of growth requires greater and greater effort on the part of the unions and more persistent support by the so-called favorable factors of union growth . . .

To compare the early and mature periods of union development on an equal basis, the concept of the saturation coefficient should be introduced. Accordingly, greater weight should be given to each per cent of growth near to the saturation point than in the 1900s when

---

27. See Bain and Price, *op. cit.*, for a fuller discussion of this point.
28. For a justification of this definition, see Bain and Price, *op. cit.*
29. An alternative way of allowing for the impact of potential union membership would have been the direct inclusion of $\Delta L^*$ as an explanatory variable. But given that the labour force figures before 1948 are derived from a linear interpolation of decennial Census of Population data, rates of change figures would be almost constant, and hence the effect of $\Delta L^*$ would be captured by the intercept of the equation.

unions represented only a negligible portion of the organizable labour force.[30]

Both the saturation effect and the reciprocal way in which the potential union membership effect is captured by the union density variable suggest that it will have a negative impact upon the rate of change of union membership. But there are also grounds for believing that union density may have a positive impact upon union growth. For as density increases from a low level, the propensity and ability to unionize may increase because employers find it more difficult to retaliate against individual union members. More important, the ability of unions to persuade employees to unionize, either because of social coercion or because of union security provisions, is likely to increase as union density increases. In short, there is an 'enforcement effect' associated with union density, and the latter may result in the former having a positive impact upon the rate of change of union membership.

Given the conflicting effects which the union density variable is meant to capture, it is not possible to say with certainty which of them will in practice be the most dominant. But even if the 'enforcement effect' predominates at lower levels of union density, it is likely to be outweighed at higher levels by the saturation effect. If this is the case, then union density will have a positive impact up to some critical level of density after which its impact will become negative. The model being specified here recognizes this possibility and allows union density to enter the equation in quadratic form. But the model also allows for linear and inverse functional forms. For it recognizes that the saturation effect may predominate at all the levels of union density observed during the period under consideration, and that its negative impact may either remain constant or decrease as union density increases.[31]

### Functional Forms and Lag Structures

The above discussion suggests that the determinants of the proportional rate of change of union membership are the proportional rate of change of retail prices, the proportional rate of change of wages, the level and/or the proportional rate of change of unemployment, and the level of union density. To put it another way, the general form of the model is

$$\Delta T = f(\Delta P, \Delta W, U, D, \epsilon)$$

30. Julius Rezler, *Union Growth Reconsidered* (New York: Kossuth Foundation, 1961), 4.
31. The linear, inverse, and quadratic relationship between $\Delta T$ and $D$ may be expressed graphically as:

where all the variables are as defined above and $\epsilon$ is a random disturbance term.

The general form of the model leaves a number of specification questions unanswered. These relate to the functional form of the relationship between the dependent variable and the explanatory variables; the lag structure of the impact of each explanatory variable upon the dependent variable; in the case of unemployment, whether it is the level, the rate of change, or both that affect the dependent variable; and, in the case of $\Delta P$ and $\Delta W$, the exact way in which these variables enter the relationship. These questions cannot be answered on *a priori* grounds in a very precise way; theory offers little more than rough guidelines. The questions are primarily of an empirical nature and can best be answered by experimenting with the data. Hence a preliminary analysis of the data was undertaken in which graphs were extensively used and regressions were run with different functional forms and lag structures.

The basic functional forms used were the linear and linear in logs. They gave very similar results, and hence only the linear form of the overall relationship is reported below. But the above *a priori* reasoning as well as the graphs suggested that density might enter the relationship in a linear, inverse, or quadratic form, and hence all these forms were

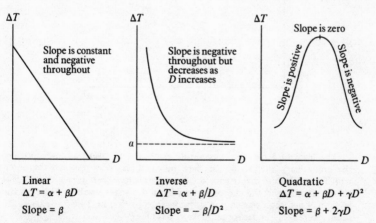

| Linear | Inverse | Quadratic |
|---|---|---|
| $\Delta T = \alpha + \beta D$ | $\Delta T = \alpha + \beta/D$ | $\Delta T = \alpha + \beta D + \gamma D^2$ |
| Slope = $\beta$ | Slope = $-\beta/D^2$ | Slope = $\beta + 2\gamma D$ |

The implication of the linear form is that all levels of $D$ have a constant negative effect upon $\Delta T$. The implication of the inverse form is that as $D$ increases, its negative effect decreases in absolute value until it reaches a given asymptote. The quadratic form implies that $D$ has a positive effect up to some critical level of density after which its effect becomes negative.

allowed for in the estimation. An examination of the graphs and the residual pattern of the preliminary regressions also suggested that the relationship between $\Delta T$ and $\Delta P$ was non-linear. More specifically, it suggested that after a certain level of $\Delta P$, its positive impact upon union growth continues but at a lower rate. Hence $\Delta PS$ was included in the model to allow for this non-linearity. It moderates the influence of price rises which are equal to or greater than 4 per cent.[32] Finally, the preliminary analysis suggested that all the explanatory variables except unemployment had an immediate impact upon $\Delta T$.[33] The detailed results are reported in the following section which discusses the estimation of the model.

32. $\Delta PS$ is a variable which shifts the slope of the relationship for observations with high values of $\Delta P$. $S$ is a dummy variable which takes the value of 1 where $P \geqslant 4$ per cent and the value of 0 for all other observations. Hence $\Delta PS$ is the multiplication of $\Delta P$ and $S$. Such a relationship can be expressed graphically as:

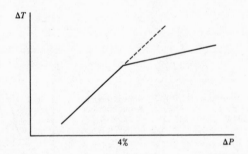

The level of 4 per cent was not determined on *a priori* grounds. Rather, the preliminary analysis of the data indicated clustered residuals associated with high values of $\Delta P$. Hence different regressions were run with different values of $\Delta PS$, and the choice was made on statistical grounds. Although the level of 4 per cent was chosen in preference to that of 3 or 5 per cent, the results were very similar for all these values of $\Delta P$.

33. Of course, union density has to be lagged one period in order to avoid introducing a spurious correlation between it and the dependent variable. See A. G. Hines, 'Trade Unions and Wage Inflation in the United Kingdom, 1893–1961', *Review of Economic Studies*, XXXI (October 1964), 238, for an explanation of this point.

## The Estimation of the Model

### The Basic Model

The above model was fitted by means of ordinary least squares to annual data for the United Kingdom for the period 1893–1970.[34] The results are given in Table 4.1.[35]

The first eight regressions in Table 4.1 employ as regressors different combinations of various specifications of prices, wages, unemployment, and union density.[36] These regressions have an explanatory power, as given by the $\bar{R}^2$, of between 61 and 73 per cent, and produce low values of *SEE* and high values of *F*. The Durbin–Watson statistic indicates that, except in the case of Regressions 1 and 8, there is no evidence of positive autocorrelation at the 1 per cent level.[37]

Taking the first five regressions, perhaps the most important finding is that the lagged rate of change of prices, $\Delta P_{t-1}$, is highly sensitive to the inclusion of the unemployment and wage regressors. When $\Delta P_{t-1}$ is included with only current prices and lagged density (Regression 1), it obtains the expected sign and is significant. When the two unemployment regressors are added (Regression 2), the '*t*' value for the $\Delta P_{t-1}$ coefficient remains significant but drops to half its previous magnitude. When $\Delta PS$ is added (Regression 3), $\Delta P_{t-1}$ picks up significance at the expense of the unemployment regressors. And when $\Delta W$ is added (Regression 4), $\Delta P_{t-1}$ not only becomes insignificant, it also changes sign. The instability of $\Delta P_{t-1}$ is caused by multicollinearity between it and most of the other explanatory variables.[38] It is incorrect to drop a variable simply to reduce multicollinearity.[39] But in the case of $\Delta P_{t-1}$,

---

34. See Appendix E for the sources and methods of compiling the data used in this study.

35. In order to test the predictive ability of the model and to assess its sensitivity to the addition of observations, the following periods of estimation were used: 1893–1965, 1893–1966, 1893–1968, and 1893–1970. The results reported in Table 4.1 are for 1893–1970, while those for other periods are given in Table 4.4. A comparison of the tables indicates that the results are similar. In regressions including $\Delta W$, the years 1939 and 1940 were omitted because of lack of data.

36. In the preliminary analysis of the data, further lags on $\Delta P$, $U$, and $\Delta W$ were used. The estimated coefficients were either insignificantly different from zero and/or had the wrong signs. The Almon lag technique was also used but the results were not satisfactory.

37. The autocorrelation may be explained in Regression 1 by the omission of serially correlated variables and in Regression 8 by the inadequacy of the inverse of union density as a regressor.

38. The correlation coefficients between $\Delta P_{t-1}$ and each of $\Delta W_t$, $U_{t-1}$, $U_{t-2}$, and $\Delta PS$ are 0.78, $-0.49$, $-0.28$, and 0.41 respectively. The full correlation matrix is given in Appendix D.

39. See above, n. 20.

TABLE 4.1

THE DETERMINANTS OF THE RATE OF CHANGE OF UNION MEMBERSHIP IN THE UNITED KINGDOM, 1893–1970

| REGRESSION | 1 | 2 | 3 | 4 | 5 | 6 | 7 | 8 | 9 | 10 | 11 |
|---|---|---|---|---|---|---|---|---|---|---|---|
| **Summary Statistics** | | | | | | | | | | | |
| $\bar{R}^2$ | 0.6075 | 0.6270 | 0.6519 | 0.6978 | 0.6750 | 0.7018 | 0.7252 | 0.6626 | 0.6948 | 0.7019 | 0.6611 |
| SEE | 4.18 | 4.07 | 3.93 | 3.71 | 3.85 | 3.69 | 3.54 | 3.92 | 3.73 | 3.69 | 3.93 |
| F | 40.2033 | 26.5499 | 24.7180 | 25.4155 | 31.7346 | 30.0286 | 28.8957 | 25.2171 | 34.6959 | 30.0391 | 29.8694 |
| df | 3, 73 | 5, 71 | 6, 70 | 7, 67 | 5, 69 | 6, 68 | 7, 67 | 6, 68 | 5, 69 | 6, 68 | 5, 69 |
| DW | 1.5032 | 1.6254 | 1.6229 | 1.6322 | 1.6467 | 1.6352 | 1.7051 | 1.5031 | 1.6578 | 1.6610 | 1.5452 |
| **Estimated Coefficients** | | | | | | | | | | | |
| Constant | 6.3207 (5.0479) | 5.6854 (3.6936) | 5.7530 (3.8682) | 6.0976 (4.2975) | 5.7616 (3.9564) | 6.0406 (4.3187) | -0.6341 (-0.2191) | -4.2898 (-3.3317) | 5.8860 (4.1732) | 1.7136 (0.5863) | -4.7942 (-3.8508) |
| $\Delta P_t$ | 0.6326 (8.5180) | 0.6141 (8.2988) | 0.7978 (7.7243) | 0.5617 (4.6869) | 0.4507 (4.9943) | 0.5831 (5.8599) | 0.5683 (5.9384) | 0.6055 (5.7368) | 0.8077 (9.9241) | 0.7708 (9.2227) | 0.8217 (9.4387) |
| $\Delta P_{t-1}$ | 0.2716 (3.5724) | 0.1660 (1.7260) | 0.2712 (2.6525) | -0.0434 (-0.3253) | | | 0.5422 (1.8799) | | | | |
| $D_{t-1}$ | -0.2018 (-5.1014) | -0.1784 (-4.4233) | -0.1756 (-4.5053) | -0.2034 (-5.3733) | -0.2022 (-5.1533) | -0.2029 (-5.4005) | | | -0.2081 (-5.4836) | 0.2513 (0.8807) | |
| $U_{t-1}$ | | -0.6222 (-2.0617) | -0.3512 (-1.1272) | -0.3992 (-1.3075) | -0.5632 (-2.1370) | -0.3506 (-1.3254) | -0.4407 (-1.7194) | -0.3447 (-1.2189) | -0.5321 (-2.1311) | -0.6223 (-2.4603) | -0.4920 (-1.8545) |
| $U_{t-2}$ | | | | 0.4413 (1.5874) | 0.6116 (2.4670) | 0.4028 (1.6119) | 0.2813 (1.1510) | 0.5136 (1.9526) | 0.5811 (2.4538) | 0.5411 (2.2993) | 0.6611 (2.6692) |
| $\Delta W_t$ | | 0.6528 (2.3660) | 0.4107 (1.4459) | 0.5020 (3.2821) | 0.3596 (3.2979) | 0.4684 (4.1814) | 0.4936 (4.5711) | 0.4233 (3.5835) | | | |
| $\Delta PS_t$ | | | -0.3794 (-2.4644) | -0.3722 (-2.4656) | | -0.3861 (-2.6856) | -0.5041 (-3.4700) | -0.3334 (-2.1739) | | | |
| $(D_{t-1})^2$ | | | | | | | -0.0135 (-2.6040) | | | -0.0083 (-1.6241) | |
| $(D_{t-1})^{-1}$ | | | | | | | | 83.6034 (4.2264) | | | 88.4206 (4.4955) |
| $\Delta(W/P)_t$ | | | | | | | | | 0.4299 (4.0088) | 0.4293 (4.0502) | 0.3974 (3.5342) |

NOTE: Figures in parentheses are estimated 't' values.

there is no *a priori* reason for including it in the equation; indeed, previous researchers have either found it to be insignificant or have not employed it at all.[40] Moreover, when an $F$ test is used to assess the improvement in fit which results from the introduction of additional regressors,[41] it reveals that $\Delta P_{t-1}$ does not improve the fit significantly.[42] Hence it was dropped from the remaining regressions.

When $\Delta P_{t-1}$ is dropped, as in Regression 6, all the coefficients of the remaining explanatory variables are significant and have the expected signs. $\Delta P_t$ has a particularly important impact upon union growth, with an increase of 1 percentage point in $\Delta P_t$ being associated with about a 0.58 percentage point increase in $\Delta T$. This result is similar to that obtained by Ashenfelter and Pencavel for the United States.[43]

But price rises do not have a constant impact upon union growth regardless of their size. $\Delta PS$ was included in the equation, as explained above,[44] to moderate the influence of price rises which are equal to or greater than 4 per cent. The magnitude of its estimated coefficient in Regression 6 is −0.39. Hence while price rises of 1, 2, and 3 per cent will be associated with increases in $\Delta T$ of 0.58, 1.16, and 1.74 per cent respectively, price rises of 4, 5, and 6 per cent will be associated with increases in $\Delta T$ of 0.76, 0.95, and 1.14 per cent respectively and not 2.32, 2.90, and 3.48 per cent respectively.[45]

The estimated coefficients of $U_{t-1}$ and $U_{t-2}$ in Regression 6 are not statistically different from each other and they possess opposite signs. This is an interesting result, indicating that it is the rate of change rather than the level of unemployment which influences union growth.[46] In effect, an increase of 1 percentage point in $\Delta U_{t-1}$ is

---

40. See Hines (1964), *op. cit.*; and Ashenfelter and Pencavel, *op. cit.*
41. See Appendix B.6 for details of this test.
42. $\Delta P_{t-1}$ contributes to the fit, but barely at the 5 per cent significance level, and only when $\Delta P$ is the only other regressor. When other regressors are included, $\Delta P_{t-1}$ does not contribute at all to the fit.
43. *op. cit.*, 441–2.
44. See p. 70.
45. When $\Delta P \geqslant 4$ per cent, the partial effect of prices is equal to $0.58 - 0.39 = 0.19$ since $S = 1$ and hence $\Delta PS = \Delta P$. When $\Delta P < 4$ per cent, the partial effect of prices is simply 0.58 since $S = 0$ and hence $\Delta PS = 0$.
46. This can be shown as follows. Assume

$$Y = \alpha + \beta X_{t-1} + \gamma X_{t-2} + \epsilon.$$

If $\gamma = -\beta$, then

$$Y = \alpha + \beta X_{t-1} - \beta X_{t-2} + \epsilon$$
$$= \alpha + \beta(X_{t-1} - X_{t-2}) + \epsilon$$
$$= \alpha + \beta(\Delta X_{t-1}) + \epsilon.$$

$U_{t-1}$ and $U_{t-2}$ were retained in the equation since they convey the same information as $\Delta U_{t-1}$ and the former exhibit more variation than the latter.

associated with about a 0.4 percentage point decrease in $\Delta T$. However, the estimated coefficients of $U_{t-1}$ and $U_{t-2}$ in Regression 6 are only significant at the 9 and 6 per cent levels respectively, and an $F$ test indicates that they make only a marginally significant improvement in the fit of the equation.[47] The marginal significance of unemployment is explained by the multicollinearity between it and $\Delta PS$. As can be seen from Regression 5, when $\Delta PS$ is excluded, the estimated coefficients of $U_{t-1}$ and $U_{t-2}$ become significant at the 1 per cent level. Since there are strong *a priori* reasons why unemployment should be related to union growth, the two unemployment regressors are retained in the model in spite of the multicollinearity problem.

$\Delta W_t$ is highly significant and has the expected sign. Regression 6 suggests that a 1 percentage point increase in $\Delta W_t$ is associated with approximately a 0.47 percentage point increase in $\Delta T$. This finding lends considerable support to the hypothesis that a 'credit effect' leads workers to unionize when money wages are rising.

The linear form of $D_{t-1}$ is used in Regression 6, the quadratic form is employed in Regression 7, and the inverse of $D_{t-1}$ is introduced in Regression 8. Regardless of which form of $D_{t-1}$ is used, its estimated coefficient is highly significant and has got the expected sign. The overall goodness of fit, as measured by the $\bar{R}^2$ and the *SEE*, is similar in all three cases, although it is slightly better for the quadratic form than for the linear and inverse. When an $F$ test is used to assess the improvement in fit which results from the introduction of additional regressors, it reveals that all three forms of $D_{t-1}$ add significantly to the fit of the equation,[48] but that the data do not distinguish between the alternative forms.

To illustrate the implications of the different functional forms of the relationship between $\Delta T$ and $D_{t-1}$, consider the following hypothetical example. On the *ceteris paribus* assumption that $\Delta P_t = \Delta W_t = 0$ and that $U_{t-1} = U_{t-2}$, let $D_{t-1}$ take the values of 10, 20, 30, 40, and 50 per cent. Table 4.2 gives the values of $\Delta T$ associated with these density levels as predicted by the three functional forms estimated by Regressions 6, 7, and 8, and these values are shown diagrammatically in Figure 4.1.

It can be seen that, other things being equal, the predicted values of $\Delta T$ associated with a 10 per cent density level are approximately 4 per cent for both the linear and inverse forms and 3.4 per cent for the quadratic form. The predicted values of $\Delta T$ continue to decline in both the linear and inverse forms, and they become negative at density levels just below 30 and 20 per cent respectively. In contrast, the predicted

47. See Appendix B.6 for the details of this test.
48. See Appendix B.6 for the details of this test.

### TABLE 4.2

### THE RATES OF CHANGE OF UNION MEMBERSHIP ASSOCIATED WITH DIFFERENT LEVELS OF UNION DENSITY

| $D_{t-1}$ (%) | Linear Form $\hat{\Delta T} = 6.0406 - 0.2029 D_{t-1}$ | | | Quadratic Form $\hat{\Delta T} = -0.6341 + 0.5422 D_{t-1} - 0.0135(D_{t-1})^2$ | | | Inverse Form $\hat{\Delta T} = -4.2898 + 83.6034(D_{t-1})^{-1}$ | | |
|---|---|---|---|---|---|---|---|---|---|
| | Constant | Density effect | $\hat{\Delta T}$ | Constant | Density effect | $\hat{\Delta T}$ | Constant | Density effect | $\hat{\Delta T}$ |
| 10 | 6.0406 | -2.0293 | 4.0113 | -0.6341 | 4.0716 | 3.4375 | -4.2898 | 8.3603 | 4.0705 |
| 20 | 6.0406 | -4.0586 | 1.9820 | -0.6341 | 5.4429 | 4.8088 | -4.2898 | 4.1802 | -0.1096 |
| 30 | 6.0406 | -6.0879 | -0.0473 | -0.6341 | 4.1141 | 3.4800 | -4.2898 | 2.7589 | -1.5309 |
| 40 | 6.0406 | -8.1172 | -2.0766 | -0.6341 | 0.0851 | -0.5490 | -4.2898 | 2.0901 | -2.1997 |
| 50 | 6.0406 | -10.1465 | -4.1059 | -0.6341 | -6.6442 | -7.2783 | -4.2898 | 1.6721 | -2.6177 |

NOTE: The density effect is calculated by substituting the given values of $D_{t-1}$ into the above equations. $\hat{\Delta T}$ is then derived by adding together the density effect and the constant.

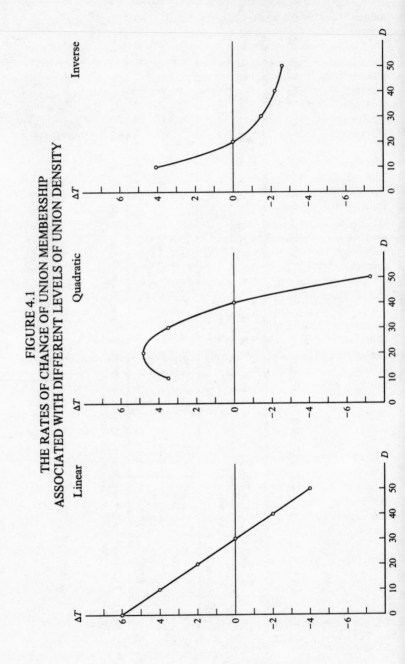

FIGURE 4.1
THE RATES OF CHANGE OF UNION MEMBERSHIP
ASSOCIATED WITH DIFFERENT LEVELS OF UNION DENSITY

values of $\Delta T$ in the quadratic form increase until they reach a peak of approximately 4.8 per cent at a density level of 20 per cent;[49] they then begin to decline and become negative at a density level just below 40 per cent. These results indicate that the quadratic form differs considerably from the other two forms. Yet the data do not distinguish between them; this suggests that most of the observations are on the downward-sloping part of the quadratic form. And a look at the $D_{t-1}$ figures reveals that this is the case; they are above the critical value of 20 per cent in every year from 1913 onwards.

## The Real Wage Variant

The results of the first eight regressions reported in Table 4.1 support the above *a priori* reasoning that prices, wages, unemployment, and union density are significant determinants of union growth. But since $\Delta P_t$ and $\Delta W_t$ are highly correlated,[50] the estimated regression coefficients of these variables may not be measuring their separate influences upon union growth. Hence an attempt was made to replace $\Delta W_t$ and $\Delta P_t$ by the ratio, $\Delta(W/P)_t$. But, as explained above,[51] the use of $\Delta(W/P)_t$ constrains the effects of $\Delta P_t$ and $\Delta W_t$ to be equal in magnitude and opposite in sign, and an $F$ test indicated that such a constraint was not valid for British data.[52] Hence the restriction imposed by using $\Delta(W/P)_t$ on its own was loosened by introducing both it and $\Delta P_t$ into the equation, with a positive sign expected for $\Delta P_t$ on the grounds that it would primarily capture the 'threat' and 'prosperity' effects and a positive sign for $\Delta(W/P)_t$ on the grounds that it would primarily reflect the 'credit effect'.

The results are given by Regressions 9, 10, and 11 of Table 4.1. They employ $\Delta P_t$, $U_{t-1}$, and $\Delta(W/P)_t$ as regressors. In addition, $D_{t-1}$ enters Regression 9 in linear form, Regression 10 in quadratic form, and Regression 11 in inverse form. These three regressions have an explanatory power, as given by the $\bar{R}^2$, of between 66 and 70 per cent. Except in the case of Regression 11, the Durbin–Watson statistic indicates that there is no evidence of positive autocorrelation at the 1 per cent significance level. All the estimated regression coefficients have the expected signs and possess reasonable magnitudes. And, with the exception of the density regressors in Regression 10, all are significantly different from zero. As in the case of the basic model, the estimated coefficients of $U_{t-1}$ and $U_{t-2}$ are not statistically different from each

49. The partial effect of $D_{t-1}$ on $\Delta T$ is equal to $0.5422 - 0.0270D_{t-1}$. It follows that if $D_{t-1}$ is approximately 20 per cent, its partial effect upon $\Delta T$ is zero. In other words, the turning point occurs at 20 per cent.
50. The correlation coefficient between $\Delta P_t$ and $\Delta W_t$ is 0.67.
51. See pp. 63–5.
52. See Appendix B.3 for details of this test.

other and possess opposite signs, indicating that it is the rate of change rather than the level of unemployment which affects union growth. And, as before, the data fail to distinguish between the linear, quadratic, and inverse forms of $D_{t-1}$.[53]

The most interesting aspect of these three regressions is provided by the estimated coefficients of $\Delta P_t$ and $\Delta(W/P)_t$. Regression 9 indicates that these are approximately 0.81 and 0.43 respectively which implies that the partial effect of prices is approximately 0.38 and that the partial effect of wages is 0.43.[54] Hence, other things being equal, Table 4.3 illustrates the effect on $\Delta T$ of some hypothetical rates of change of $\Delta P_t$ and $\Delta W_t$. For example, the second row of the table indicates that if money wages were to increase by 1 percentage point while prices were constant ($\Delta P_t = 0$), then there would be a 0.43 percentage point increase in the rate of change of union membership. In general, it can be seen from Table 4.3 that $\Delta T$ increases not only when real wages are falling but also when they are constant or rising. This finding is consistent with the hypothesis that workers are led to unionize not only by the 'threat' and 'prosperity' effects but also by the 'credit effect'.

These findings confirm the results of the basic model. A comparison of Regressions 6 and 9 reveals that all the relevant regression coefficients are more or less the same and that the two regressions are basically similar. It is particularly noteworthy that regardless of whether prices and wages are introduced into the equation as two separate variables as in Regression 6, or in the form of the ratio, $\Delta(W/P)_t$. as in Regression 9, the magnitude of the partial effects of $\Delta P_t$ and $\Delta W_t$ upon $\Delta T$ are similar. Moreover, $\Delta P_t$ has virtually the same estimated coefficient regardless of whether it enters the equation on its own as in Regression 2, or in company with $\Delta W_t$ as in Regression 6. The similarity of the results suggests that any multicollinearity which may exist in the basic model is not of harmful degree. And, given the *a priori* reasons advanced above for preferring the basic model, attention can therefore be concentrated on it rather than on the real wage variant.

53. Lags were allowed for on $\Delta(W/P)_t$, and the Almon lag technique was also used. In addition, the positive and negative changes in $\Delta(W/P)_t$ were employed as separate regressors in an attempt to allow for the possibility that the effects of real wages upon union growth may differ depending upon whether they are increasing or decreasing. But, in all cases, the results proved to be unsatisfactory.

54. For purposes of illustration, write the estimated equation as

$$\widehat{\Delta T} = B + 0.81\Delta P + 0.43(\Delta W - \Delta P)$$

where $B$ represents the contribution of all the other variables in the model. Then the partial effect of $\Delta P$ is $\delta \Delta T/\delta \Delta P = 0.81 - 0.43 = 0.38$, while that of $\Delta W$ is 0.43.

## TABLE 4.3
## THE RATES OF CHANGE OF UNION MEMBERSHIP ASSOCIATED
## WITH DIFFERENT RATES OF CHANGE OF PRICES AND WAGES

| Case | $\Delta P_t$ | $\Delta W_t$ | $\Delta T_t$ |
|---|---|---|---|
| Constant money wages and rising prices | 1 | 0 | 0.38 |
| Rising money wages and constant prices | 0 | 1 | 0.43 |
| Money wages and prices rising at the same rate | 1 | 1 | 0.81 |
| Prices rising at a higher rate than money wages | 2 | 1 | 1.19 |
| Money wages rising at a higher rate than prices | 1 | 2 | 1.24 |

### Structural Shifts, Data Sensitivity, and Predictions

The model of union growth which has been estimated above is clearly satisfactory when judged by the criterion of overall goodness of fit as well as in terms of the signs, magnitudes, and significance of the estimated regression coefficients. The model was subjected to additional tests, however, to determine whether there are any structural shifts in the relationship which the model describes, whether it is sensitive to the addition of observations, and whether it is able to make accurate predictions.

The model is estimated over a period of almost eighty years, and there could easily have been changes during that period in the structure of the relationship which the model describes. For example, a structural shift might have occurred around such years as 1922 and 1933. The early 1920s saw the onset of the post-war depression, a severe erosion of the membership gains made by unions during the previous decade, and the withdrawal of Southern Ireland from the United Kingdom which affected not only the structure of the economy but also the internal consistency of many of the statistical series used in this study. After 1933, the depression began to ease and the trade union movement regained lost ground and established itself in new industries and occupations. Hence the overall period was first divided into the sub-periods, 1893–1921 and 1922–70, and the Chow test was applied. Then the overall period was divided into two different sub-periods, 1893–1932 and 1933–70, and the Chow test was applied again. In both instances, the test indicated that there had not been a structural shift.[55]

55. In effect, the Chow test indicated that the magnitudes of the estimated regression coefficients of the explanatory variables were similar regardless of the period of estimation. See Appendix B.4 for the details of the test.

TABLE 4.4

THE DETERMINANTS OF THE RATE OF CHANGE OF UNION
MEMBERSHIP IN THE UNITED KINGDOM, 1893–1965,
1893–1966, 1893–1968, and 1893–1970

| REGRESSION | 1<br>1893–1965 | 2<br>1893–1966 | 3<br>1893–1968 | 4<br>1893–1970 |
|---|---|---|---|---|
| Summary<br>Statistics | | | | |
| $\bar{R}^2$ | 0.7292 | 0.7274 | 0.7282 | 0.7252 |
| SEE | 3.62 | 3.61 | 3.56 | 3.54 |
| F | 27.5426 | 27.6850 | 28.5621 | 28.8957 |
| df | 7, 62 | 7, 63 | 7, 65 | 7, 67 |
| DW | 1.7358 | 1.7221 | 1.7161 | 1.7051 |
| Estimated<br>Coefficients | | | | |
| Constant | −1.0120<br>(−0.3401) | −0.9878<br>(−0.3328) | −0.9758<br>(−0.3335) | −0.6341<br>(−0.2191) |
| $\Delta P_t$ | 0.5801<br>(5.8957) | 0.5731<br>(5.8622) | 0.5705<br>(5.9267) | 0.5683<br>(5.9384) |
| $D_{t-1}$ | 0.5942<br>(1.9927) | 0.5901<br>(1.9844) | 0.5881<br>(2.0078) | 0.5422<br>(1.8799) |
| $(D_{t-1})^2$ | −0.0144<br>(−2.6823) | −0.0144<br>(−2.6877) | −0.0144<br>(−2.7306) | −0.0135<br>(−2.6040) |
| $U_{t-1}$ | −0.4591<br>(−1.7405) | −0.4608<br>(−1.7517) | −0.4656<br>(−1.7997) | −0.4407<br>(−1.7194) |
| $U_{t-2}$ | 0.2765<br>(1.1027) | 0.2828<br>(1.1311) | 0.2905<br>(1.1814) | 0.2813<br>(1.1510) |
| $\Delta PS_t$ | −0.5356<br>(−3.5497) | −0.5193<br>(−3.4814) | −0.5128<br>(−3.5042) | −0.5041<br>(−3.4699) |
| $\Delta W_t$ | 0.4842<br>(4.3565) | 0.4825<br>(4.3532) | 0.4812<br>(4.4075) | 0.4936<br>(4.5711) |

NOTE: Figures in parentheses are estimated '*t*' values.

Table 4.4 suggests that the model is not sensitive to the addition of
observations. The table presents the results of the basic model, using
the quadratic form of $D_{t-1}$, for different periods of estimation.[56] A

56. The results were also similar regardless of the period of estimation when the
linear and inverse forms of $D_{t-1}$ were used.

quick glance at the four regressions suggests that they are basically similar regardless of the period for which they are estimated. This visual assessment of the model's stability is confirmed by the appropriate $F$ test.[57] The model's insensitivity to the addition of observations provides further support for the view that any multicollinearity which is present is harmless.[58]

The model's predictive ability can be assessed by examining Figures 4.2 and 4.3 which show the predicted and actual values of $\Delta T$ for 1893–1970. The predictions in Figure 4.2 were made by using the estimated regression equation for 1893–1965 (Regression 1 in Table 4.4), while those in Figure 4.3 were made by using the estimated regression equation for 1893–1968 (Regression 3 in Table 4.4). Thus the predictions in Figure 4.2 for 1893–1965 and in Figure 4.3 for 1893–1968 are inside the sample period, and their main value lies in demonstrating that the residuals of the estimated equations present no cause for concern.[59] The predictions in Figure 4.2 for 1966–70 and in Figure 4.3 for 1969–70 lie outside the sample period, and they indicate that the model predicts reasonably well. This visual assessment is confirmed by Theil's Inequality Coefficient.[60] The overall coefficient was reasonably low (0.47). More important, the bias and variance components of the coefficient were close to zero while the covariance component was close to unity. Since little can be done about inequality in the covariance component, the sources of forecasting error which the investigator can improve upon are few. In short, the model's predictive ability is quite satisfactory.

## Conclusion

This chapter has specified a model of union growth and estimated it using data for the United Kingdom for the period 1893–1970. It

57. See Appendix B.5 for details of this test.
58. See Kmenta, *loc. cit.*, and Koutsoyiannis, *op. cit.*, on this point.
59. Nor were any weaknesses in the specification of the model revealed when the residuals were analysed by more systematic methods. See P. Rao and R. L. Miller, *Applied Econometrics* (Belmont, California: Wandsworth, 1971), 112–21, for a description of the methods used.
60. The closer the inequality coefficient is to zero the better the predictions. The coefficient can be decomposed into three inequality components known as the bias, variance, and covariance proportions. If the bias and variance proportions make up a large part of the inequality coefficient, the investigator can improve the quality of the predictions by respecifying the model. But if the major part of the inequality coefficient is made up of the covariance proportion, then the predictive ability of the model cannot be significantly improved upon. See Appendix C for details of Theil's Inequality Coefficient.

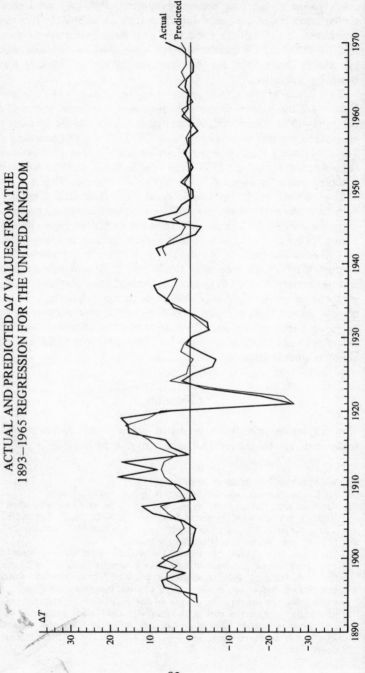

FIGURE 4.2
ACTUAL AND PREDICTED Δ*T* VALUES FROM THE
1893−1965 REGRESSION FOR THE UNITED KINGDOM

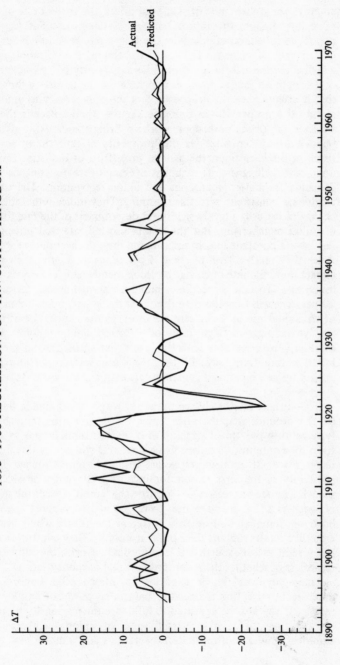

*Conclusion*

FIGURE 4.3
ACTUAL AND PREDICTED $\Delta T$ VALUES FROM THE
1893–1968 REGRESSION FOR THE UNITED KINGDOM

83

employs the current rate of change of prices, the current rate of change of money wages, the rate of change of unemployment lagged one period, and the level of union density lagged one period as determinants of the rate of change of union membership. It also employs terms which allow the effects of prices and union density to be non-linear.

The rate of change of prices is included in the model on the grounds that it affects both the propensity and the opportunity to unionize. It affects the propensity to unionize via the 'threat effect': the effect which rising prices have upon workers' living standards. It affects the opportunity to unionize via the 'prosperity effect': the effect which rising prices have upon the general prosperity of industry, and hence upon the willingness and ability of employers to concede worker demands for better conditions and union recognition. The empirical results are consistent with this reasoning. They indicate that the rate of change of prices is a highly significant determinant of the rate of change of union membership. But the results also indicate that price rises do not have a constant impact upon union growth regardless of their size. After they reach a level of about 4 per cent per annum, their positive impact upon the rate of change of union membership continues but at a lower rate. To take a specific example, an annual average price rise of 20 per cent will have less than five times the impact upon union growth of an annual rise of 4 per cent. In short, as the experience of the past few years suggests, high rates of inflation tend to numb people's sensitivity to price rises with the result that an increase in the annual inflation rate from, say, 15 to 20 per cent has proportionately less impact upon the national consciousness than an increase from, say, 3 to 4 per cent.

The current rate of change of money wages is included in the model on the grounds that the price variable does not necessarily by itself fully capture the 'threat effect'. For if workers think in real as distinct from money terms, then their living standards will not be threatened by rising prices if money wages are rising faster. Allowing for this possibility is the first reason for including the wage variable in the model. The second reason is to capture the 'credit effect': the tendency of workers to credit wage rises to unions and to support them in the hope of doing as well or even better in the future. Once again, the empirical results support the *a priori* reasoning. They confirm that there is a 'credit effect' and that it is quite distinct from the 'threat effect' regardless of whether the latter is seen in real or money terms.

Unemployment can be expected to influence the opportunity to unionize by affecting the relative bargaining power of employers and unions. It can also be expected to influence the propensity to unionize by affecting the relative attractiveness of union membership. The empirical results confirm these expectations and indicate that it is the rate of change of unemployment lagged one period which has the most significant impact upon the rate of change of union membership.

The lagged level of union density is included in the model for three reasons. First, to allow for the impact which potential union membership has upon union growth. Second, to capture the 'saturation effect': the greater difficulty of further increasing union membership as union density rises, partly because there are fewer workers left to recruit and partly because those who are left have less propensity and/or ability to unionize. And third, to capture the 'enforcement effect': the greater ease of further increasing union membership as union density rises, partly because employers find it more difficult to retaliate against individual union members and, partly because unions find it easier to apply social coercion and union security provisions. Since it is not possible to say with certainty which of these conflicting effects will in practice predominate and hence what the functional form of the relationship will be, the model allows the lagged level of union density to enter the relationship in linear and non-linear forms. The data do not discriminate between the different functional forms, but the results indicate that all of them are highly significant determinants of the rate of change of union membership.

The model is clearly satisfactory when judged in terms of the usual criterion of overall goodness of fit as well as in terms of the signs, magnitudes, and significance of the estimated regression coefficients. It is also satisfactory when judged in terms of its structural stability, data sensitivity, and predictive ability.

But most of the variables included in the model are primarily economic in nature, and hence it might be seen as unsatisfactory on the grounds that it ignores the various socio-political factors which previous writers have suggested as being important determinants of union growth. In fact, an attempt was made to test for the impact of these factors upon the rate of change of union membership. A political variable similar to that used by Ashenfelter and Pencavel for the United States was included in the model: the percentage of members in the House of Commons who could be broadly defined as 'labour supporters'. In addition, since the periods 1915—20 and 1940—5 were characterized by compulsory arbitration and other measures which produced a social climate particularly favourable to trade unions, dummy variables which took the value of unity during these periods and zero for all other years were included in the model.[61] Finally, since the Gallup Polls have produced data from 1952 onwards on the public attitude towards unions by asking a national sample of the population

---

61. For a discussion of these periods, see G. S. Bain, *The Growth of White-Collar Unionism* (Oxford: Clarendon Press, 1970), 142—5 and 155—8.

the question – 'Generally speaking, and thinking of Britain as a whole, do you think trade unions are a good thing or a bad thing?' – the model was run for the period 1952–70 including as a variable the proportion of the sample who thought that trade unions were a 'good thing'.[62]

In all cases, the results were unsatisfactory. The estimated co-efficients of these variables either had the wrong sign, lacked significance, or were faulty in both respects. Of course, this does not prove, nor is it meant to imply, that socio-political factors have no impact upon union growth. The above variables may be, and some at least almost certainly are, poor proxies for the factors they are attempting to measure. Regardless of how adequate these proxies are, the socio-political factors may have an indirect impact upon union growth which is captured by the economic variables which are included in the model. And given the 'voluntary principle' upon which the British industrial relations system has traditionally been based, it may be that the impact of such factors as the law and government action has not been sufficiently general or pervasive to be reflected by union growth at aggregate level; their impact may be apparent only in particular industries and occupations. Be that as it may, the results presented in this chapter suggest that there is no need to make separate allowance for the socio-political determinants of union growth in a model which is attempting to account for the rate of change in aggregate union membership in the United Kingdom. That this is not the case for all countries, however, will be shown in the following chapter.

62. See *ibid.*, 88–9.

# 5
# International Comparisons

The nature of the trade union movement and the industrial relations system in which it operates varies from one country to another. Hence a model which has been estimated on the basis of data for the United Kingdom is unlikely to apply without modification to other countries. But, in as much as the model's specification rests upon arguments of a general nature, its basic hypotheses should hold for countries with broadly similar industrial relations systems. This chapter tests the general validity of the model's basic hypotheses by attempting to apply them to the United States, Australia, and Sweden.

### United States

Only one modification needs to be made to the basic model developed in the previous chapter in applying it to the United States. Whereas there was no need to make separate allowance for the impact of socio-political factors upon aggregate union growth in the United Kingdom, there is such a need in the case of the United States, for government action has had a most significant impact upon aggregate union growth in that country.

There are good reasons for suggesting that the government's influence upon union growth was most favourable in the United States between 1937 and 1947. The Supreme Court upheld the constitutionality of the Wagner Act in 1937, and there can be little doubt that it bolstered union membership over the next few years. There can also be little doubt that the War Labor Board promoted union growth throughout the war by inserting into collective agreements such devices as maintenance of membership clauses, the check-off, and grievance procedures with arbitration. As the war came to an end, however, the government's attitude to unions became less favourable. And in 1947 the federal government passed the Taft-Hartley Act and twenty-six state governments implemented similar legislation designed to restrict union growth and power.[1]

Hence the basic model of union growth has been modified for the United States by including in it a dummy variable, $G$, which takes the value of unity for the period 1937–47 and zero for all other years. The modified model was then fitted by means of the ordinary least squares technique to annual data for the period 1897–1970. The results are given in Table 5.1.

The only difference between the first three regressions in Table 5.1 is that $D_{t-1}$ enters Regression 1 in linear form, Regression 2 in quadratic form, and Regression 3 in inverse form. Regression 3 clearly produces the best results. It has the highest $\bar{R}^2$, the lowest value of SEE, and the highest value of $F$. In addition, the Durbin–Watson statistic is inconclusive for Regression 3, whereas it indicates the existence of positive autocorrelation in Regressions 1 and 2. And an $F$ test indicates that the inverse form of $D_{t-1}$ makes a more significant improvement in the fit of the equation than the linear or quadratic forms.[2] Hence the discussion focuses on Regression 3.

A quick glance at the summary statistics of Regression 3 shows the satisfactory nature of the results. The $\bar{R}^2$ indicates that 69 per cent of the variation in $\Delta T$ is explained by the regressors employed. The standard error of the estimate is low, and the large magnitude of the $F$ statistic indicates the overall significance of the regression. The only unsatisfactory result is the inconclusiveness of the Durbin–Watson statistic.

The estimated coefficient of $\Delta W_t$ is highly significant. Its magnitude implies that, other things being equal, a 1 percentage point increase in money wages would lead to a 0.7 percentage point increase in $\Delta T$. And

1. For the details of the various pieces of legislation and the way in which they influenced union growth, see, for example, Irving Bernstein, *The New Deal Collective Bargaining Policy* (Berkeley: University of California Press, 1950); and Philip Ross, *The Government as a Source of Union Power* (Providence: Brown University Press, 1965). A brief but useful summary can be found in Orme W. Phelps, *Introduction to Labor Economics* (New York: McGraw-Hill, 1961), 152–89.
2. See Appendix B.6 for details of this test. In fact, the quadratic form is rejected for the United States because the magnitudes and signs of the density regressors imply that the relationship between $\Delta T$ and $D_{t-1}$ is of the form

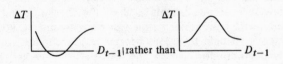

TABLE 5.1

## THE DETERMINANTS OF THE RATE OF CHANGE OF UNION MEMBERSHIP IN THE UNITED STATES, 1897–1970

| REGRESSION | 1<br>1897–1970 | 2<br>1897–1970 | 3<br>1897–1970 | 4<br>1897–1968 | 5<br>1897–1965 |
|---|---|---|---|---|---|
| Summary Statistics | | | | | |
| $\bar{R}^2$ | 0.5284 | 0.6385 | 0.6860 | 0.6853 | 0.6860 |
| SEE | 6.1615 | 5.3944 | 5.0277 | 5.0947 | 5.1802 |
| F | 14.6097 | 19.3083 | 27.3782 | 26.5713 | 25.5585 |
| df | 6, 65 | 7, 64 | 6, 65 | 6, 63 | 6, 60 |
| DW | 0.9903 | 1.2556 | 1.4316 | 1.4341 | 1.4219 |
| Estimated Coefficients | | | | | |
| Constant | 11.9983<br>(6.0610) | 30.1501<br>(6.9452) | −7.4913<br>(−5.1810) | −7.3668<br>(−4.9471) | −7.3594<br>(−4.6288) |
| $\Delta W_t$ | 0.7378<br>(4.1387) | 0.6334<br>(4.0158) | 0.7053<br>(4.8528) | 0.7066<br>(4.7886) | 0.7059<br>(4.6998) |
| $\Delta P_{t-1}$ | 0.4822<br>(2.6536) | 0.6113<br>(3.7833) | 0.5431<br>(3.6623) | 0.5460<br>(3.6311) | 0.5497<br>(3.5937) |
| $\Delta U_t^+$ | −0.1001<br>(−2.3753) | −0.0917<br>(−2.4819) | −0.0775<br>(−2.2778) | −0.0794<br>(−2.2834) | −0.0800<br>(−2.2354) |
| $\Delta U_t^-$ | 0.0763<br>(4.0354) | 0.0604<br>(3.5673) | 0.0727<br>(4.7907) | 0.0734<br>(4.7513) | 0.0739<br>(4.6773) |
| Dummy $G$ | 6.7632<br>(3.2247) | 9.5296<br>(4.9279) | 8.2208<br>(4.7534) | 8.1551<br>(4.6277) | 8.1613<br>(4.5137) |
| $(D_{t-1})^{-1}$ | | | 122.3410<br>(9.3571) | 121.7440<br>(9.1217) | 121.8780<br>(8.8190) |
| $D_{t-1}$ | −0.5374<br>(−6.0480) | −3.1889<br>(−5.4365) | | | |
| $(D_{t-1})^2$ | | 0.0714<br>(4.5606) | | | |

NOTE: Figures in parentheses are estimated '$t$' values.

this result suggests that the 'credit effect' is an important factor in the American workers' decision to become and to remain a union member.

The price regressor is $\Delta P_{t-1}$ and its estimated coefficient is highly significant.[3] Its magnitude implies that, other things being equal, a 1 percentage point increase in $\Delta P_{t-1}$ would lead to a 0.54 percentage point increase in $\Delta T$.

The unemployment regressors used in the American regressions are $\Delta U_t^+$ and $\Delta U_t^-$.[4] In a year in which the level of unemployment is increasing, $\Delta U^+$ takes as its value the size of $\Delta U$ in that year whereas $\Delta U^-$ is set equal to zero. In a year in which the level of unemployment is decreasing, $\Delta U^-$ takes as its value the size of $\Delta U$ in that year and $\Delta U^+$ is set equal to zero. The arguments advanced about unemployment in the previous chapter suggest that $\Delta U^-$ will have a positive impact upon union growth while $\Delta U^+$ will have a negative impact.

The two unemployment regressors obtain the expected signs and are significantly different from zero. The magnitude of their effects upon union growth is small and similar. $\Delta U^-$ is more significant than $\Delta U^+$ which suggests that the tendency for workers to join unions when unemployment is decreasing is a more significant determinant of changes in union membership than the tendency for them to leave unions when unemployment is increasing.

The alternative formulations of $D_{t-1}$ are all highly significant, indicating that the higher the level of union density the more difficult it is to secure further increases in $\Delta T$. But, as was indicated above, the inverse form gives the best results in terms of overall summary statistics. This suggests that, other things being equal, as the level of density increases $\Delta T$ will decrease but at a decreasing rate.[5] Such a conclusion contrasts with the findings of Ashenfelter and Pencavel for the United States[6] which suggest that the data do not distinguish between the various formulations of $D_{t-1}$.

3. The $\Delta P_{t-1}$ regressor was preferred to $\Delta P_t$ on empirical grounds. Further, the $\Delta PS$ regressor employed for the United Kingdom was found to be insignificant for the United States. And the ratio $\Delta(W/P)$ also gave unsatisfactory results for the United States.

4. Both the level and the rate of change of unemployment were used and different lag structures were allowed for, but the results were not satisfactory.

5. See above, p. 68, n. 31.

6. Ashenfelter and Pencavel define the density concept as total trade union membership as a percentage of 'unionizable' employment, whereas it is defined here as total union membership as a percentage of the total labour force excluding employers, the self-employed, and members of the armed forces but including the unemployed. Further, the estimation period is shorter for the Ashenfelter and Pencavel study. See Orley Ashenfelter and John H. Pencavel, 'American Trade Union Growth: 1900–1960', *Quarterly Journal of Economics*, LXXXIII (August 1969), 442–3.

The government's impact upon union growth during the 1930s and 1940s, as represented by the dummy variable $G$, is highly significant. The results imply that, if all other things were equal, $\Delta T$ would be 8 percentage points higher in a year falling within the period 1937–47 than in a year falling outside this period.

Regressions 4 and 5 give the results of the preferred equation when it is estimated for periods of various length. The similarity of the results suggests that the model is not sensitive to the addition of observations, and this is confirmed by the appropriate $F$ test. The predictions obtained from Regression 5 are presented in Figure 5.1. The graph indicates that the model's predictive ability is satisfactory, and this is confirmed by Theil's Inequality Coefficient.[7]

Finally, the model was evaluated in relation to that developed for the United States by Ashenfelter and Pencavel. For this purpose, three equations were fitted to American data for the period 1904–60: the Ashenfelter–Pencavel equation, the Bain–Elsheikh equation, and a hybrid which includes all the variables used in the previous two equations.[8] The results are given in Table 5.2.

A comparison of Regressions 1 and 2 in Table 5.2 indicates that although the Bain–Elsheikh model uses fewer explanatory variables than the Ashenfelter–Pencavel model, the former produces results at least as good as those of the latter. An examination of the hybrid equation, Regression 3, indicates that the Bain–Elsheikh model is actually preferable to that estimated by Ashenfelter and Pencavel. For, with the exception of the coefficients of $\Delta E^*_{t-1}$ and $\Delta E^*_{t-2}$, those of all the other regressors employed in the Ashenfelter–Pencavel model are insignificant. Moreover, $\Delta P_t$, $|U^P_t|$ and $(T/E^*)^{-1}_{t-1}$ appear with the wrong sign. In contrast, $\Delta U^+_t$ is the only regressor employed in the Bain–Elsheikh model which appears with an insignificant coefficient.[9]

A final point in comparing the two models concerns the data they use. Since they employ different price and union membership data, both models were fitted to both sets of data. Whereas the Ashenfelter–Pencavel model gives less favourable results when fitted to the data used in the Bain–Elsheikh model, the latter performs equally well on both

7. See Appendix C for details of Theil's Inequality Coefficient.
8. The hybrid equation includes fourteen regressors, and hence it runs the risk of suffering from serious multicollinearity. But since the purpose is merely to compare the two models, and since multicollinearity is a matter of degree, it was felt that the results were of some interest. The authors are indebted to Professor Pencavel for suggesting this procedure.
9. The coefficient of $\Delta U^+_t$ is insignificant not only in the hybrid equation but also in the Bain–Elsheikh equation when it is estimated for the period 1904–60 (Regression 2). It is significant, however, when the equation is estimated over longer periods (see Table 5.1).

FIGURE 5.1
ACTUAL AND PREDICTED Δ*T* VALUES FROM THE
1897–1965 REGRESSION FOR THE UNITED STATES

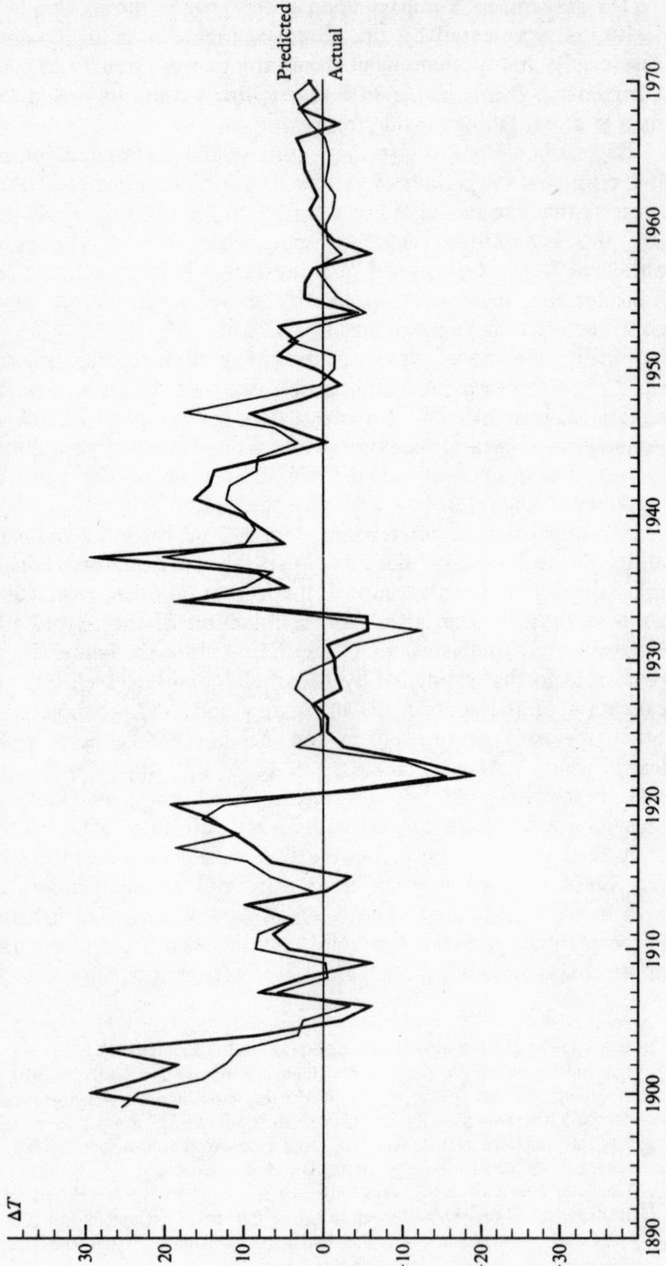

## TABLE 5.2
## A COMPARISON OF THE ASHENFELTER–PENCAVEL AND THE BAIN–ELSHEIKH MODELS FOR THE UNITED STATES, 1904–1960

| | Ashenfelter–Pencavel Equation (1) | Bain–Elsheikh Equation (2) | Hybrid Equation (3) |
|---|---|---|---|
| **Summary Statistics** | | | |
| $\bar{R}^2$ | 0.7128 | 0.7053 | 0.7331 |
| SEE | 3.80 | 4.38 | 4.20 |
| F | 24.1651 | 23.9036 | 13.8195 |
| df | 6, 50 | 6, 50 | 12, 44 |
| DW | 1.6406 | 1.6138 | 1.8963 |
| **Estimated Coefficients** | | | |
| Constant | −15.2315 (−4.9470) | −7.7307 (−4.0988) | −9.3757 (−2.3678) |
| $\Delta E_t^*$ | 0.1264 (1.5618) | | 0.1037 (0.8021) |
| $\Delta E_{t-1}^*$ | 0.1080 (2.2550) | | 0.1744 (2.5133) |
| $\Delta E_{t-2}^*$ | 0.0808 (1.7856) | | 0.1806 (2.1814) |
| $\Delta E_{t-3}^*$ | 0.0448 (1.3040) | | 0.1225 (1.8095) |
| $\Delta P_t$ | 0.6798 (5.2094) | | −0.0577 (−0.2317) |
| $\Delta P_{t-1}$ | | 0.4605 (3.4501) | 0.3745 (2.0503) |
| $\Delta W_t$ | | 0.7523 (5.8943) | 0.7499 (2.9620) |
| $U_t^P$ | 0.2960 (3.6538) | | −0.0245 (−0.1459) |
| $\Delta U_t^{+}$ | | −0.0372 (−1.1722) | −0.0021 (−0.0562) |
| $\Delta U_t^{-}$ | | 0.0582 (4.2505) | 0.0549 (3.3901) |
| $G_t$ (Democrats) | 0.2150 (3.8393) | | 0.0375 (0.4975) |
| $G_t$ (Dummy) | | 8.6261 (5.4611) | 5.6615 (2.6183) |
| $(T/E^*)_{t-1}^{-1}$ | 67.7200 (2.1384) | | −178.1130 (−1.3131) |
| $(D_{t-1})^{-1}$ | | 101.0300 (4.9640) | 182.4000 (2.3771) |

NOTE: Figures in parentheses are estimated '$t$' values.

sets of data. In short, the Bain–Elsheikh model is more robust in the sense that it is less sensitive to the data employed.[10]

## Australia

In the case of Australia, as in that of the United States, the basic model developed in the previous chapter must be modified to allow for the impact of government action upon union growth. For Australia is unique in the extent to which it relies upon compulsory arbitration. And most commentators are agreed that the economic gains and legal protection accruing to workers and their unions under the arbitration system have provided a powerful stimulus to the growth of Australian unions.[11] This was particularly so in the early days of the system when, as Oxnam has noted, 'low-paid groups of workers who were formerly without union organization or were members of weak unions could, by registering under arbitration law, compel their employers to negotiate before an industrial tribunal and thereby obtain wages and conditions comparable to those which the stronger unions had been able to obtain by direct negotiation.'[12]

Hence, in applying the basic model of union growth to Australia, a dummy variable $C$ was included in the model to allow for the favourable impact of compulsory arbitration upon union growth during the early years of the twentieth century. Since the compulsory arbitration system took shape between the years 1896 and 1912, there is no problem in allowing its impact to begin in 1907, the first year for

10. Since the Bain–Elsheikh model performs equally well on both sets of data, the question of which set is best need not arise. But the set used in the Bain–Elsheikh model is preferred because, for example, its trade union membership series excludes Canadian members from 1910 onwards whereas the Ashenfelter–Pencavel series excludes them only from 1930 onwards.

   Similarly, the trade union membership series used in the Bain–Elsheikh model is preferred to that compiled by the Bureau of Labor Statistics for the reasons given in G. S. Bain and R. J. Price, *Profiles of Union Growth* (Oxford: Blackwell, forthcoming). When the model was fitted to the BLS data, however, the signs, magnitudes, and significance of the estimated coefficients were similar. But the summary statistics of the regressions were not as good when BLS data were used.

11. See, for example, Ian G. Sharpe, 'The Growth of Australian Trade Unions: 1907–1969', *Journal of Industrial Relations*, XIII (June 1971), 140–41; K. F. Walker, 'White-Collar Unionism in Australia', *White-Collar Trade Unions*, ed. Adolf Sturmthal (Urbana: University of Illinois Press, 1966), 9–10; and D. W. Oxnam, 'Industrial Arbitration in Australia: Its Effects on Wages and Unions', *Industrial and Labor Relations Review*, IX (July 1956), 617–18.

12. *op. cit.*, 617.

which the model is estimated. But there is no way of determining *a priori* when this factor ceased to influence the rate of change of union membership, and hence, following Sharpe's example, the year 1913 has been arbitrarily chosen. In other words, *C* is defined to equal the value of unity from 1907 to 1913 and zero thereafter.

There is also reason to |believe that the arbitration system has influenced union growth by the manner in which it has regulated wages. In 1907 the Commonwealth Court of Conciliation and Arbitration laid down in the famous 'Harvester' judgment what in its opinion was a 'living' or 'basic' wage. In 1914 it began the practice of maintaining the 'basic wage' in real terms by adjusting the Harvester standard in accordance with changes in the retail price index. These cost-of-living adjustments were initially made on an annual basis, but in 1921 a system of automatic quarterly adjustments was instituted. While the federal tribunal discontinued the automatic cost-of-living adjustments in 1953, some of the state tribunals did not. And in 1961 the federal tribunal retreated somewhat from its 1953 decision by indicating that in future it would change the basic wage in proportion to changes in the retail price index as long as industry had the capacity to pay.[13] In short, the basic wage in Australia has tended to be closely tied to the retail price index in one way or another for over fifty years.

In as much as the arbitration system has reduced the threat which rising prices pose for the workers' standard of living, $\Delta P$ is unlikely to be an important determinant of union growth in Australia. Given that the 'threat effect' is largely absent, $\Delta P$ and $\Delta T$ will be related only to the extent that the 'prosperity effect' is operative and is captured by the price variable. The arbitration system may also have reduced the importance of the 'credit effect'. For if workers perceive their wage rises as stemming from the decisions of an official tribunal, they may be less inclined to give unions credit for them. But the 'credit effect' is unlikely to disappear altogether. For unions are likely to claim the credit for all wage rises and to use them as an argument for persuading workers to unionize. As one historian has noted,

What happened in the early days of industrial arbitration was that the officials of a union, having obtained an award which raised wages and improved conditions all round, would go through the country and say

13. For a history of the basic wage see J. E. Isaac and G. W. Ford, *Australian Labour Economics: Readings* (Melbourne: Sun Books, 1967), 6–14; K. J. Hancock, 'The Basic Wage and The Cost of Living', *Australian Economic Papers*, I (September 1962), 42–56; and K. F. Walker, *Australian Industrial Relations Systems* (Cambridge, Mass.: Harvard University Press, 1970), 102–16.

to the workers in their craft or industry: 'See what we have done for you'. The men could not stand out.[14]

And since the industrial tribunals have tended not only to maintain the real basic wage but also, following representations from trade unions, to increase it periodically, the 'credit effect' has probably continued into more recent times.

Bearing these points in mind, the basic model, as modified by the inclusion of the dummy variable *C*, was fitted by the ordinary least squares technique to annual data for the period 1907–69. The results are given in Table 5.3.

A quick glance at the results indicates that they are satisfactory. The three regressions have an explanatory power, as measured by the $\bar{R}^2$, of over 72 per cent and produce low values of *SEE* and high values of *F*. In all cases, the Durbin–Watson statistic is inconclusive. All the estimated regression coefficients have the expected signs, possess reasonable magnitudes, and, with one exception, are significantly different from zero.[15]

The one exception is $\Delta P_t$. Its estimated coefficient is not significantly different from zero, and an *F* test indicates that the inclusion of this variable in the equation does not significantly improve the fit.[16] The same is true when lagged values of $\Delta P$ are used. And if $\Delta PS$ is introduced it obtains the wrong sign and is insignificant. The price variable's lack of significance comes as no surprise. It merely confirms that the 'threat effect' is largely absent in Australia due to the workings of the compulsory arbitration system, and it suggests that the 'prosperity effect' is of little importance or is not captured by the price variable.[17]

14. W. K. Hancock, *Australia* (London: Ernest Benn, 1945), 181.
15. The density regressors' coefficients in Regression 3 are insignificant. But given the significance of density in the other regressions and the similarity between the estimated coefficients in the three regressions, the insignificance of these coefficients is explicable in terms of multicollinearity. The correlation coefficient between $D_{t-1}$ and its square is 0.9869. Hence it is not possible to draw any conclusions about the adequacy of the quadratic form.
16. See Appendix B.6 for details of the test.
17. Given that the correlation coefficient between $\Delta P$ and $\Delta W$ is high (0.657), it might be argued that the price variable's insignificance is explained by the presence of multicollinearity. But the results obtained by using $\Delta(W/P)$, either on its own or in conjunction with $\Delta P$, were also unsatisfactory. The same was true when various lag structures were applied to $\Delta(W/P)$. Although Sharpe obtained satisfactory results with $\Delta(W/P)$, his wage and price series were different from those employed here. And, on the basis of the data employed in the present study, an *F* test indicated that the constraint imposed by using $\Delta(W/P)$ is invalid.

## TABLE 5.3
## THE DETERMINANTS OF THE RATE OF CHANGE OF UNION MEMBERSHIP IN AUSTRALIA, 1907–1969

| REGRESSION | 1 | 2 | 3 |
|---|---|---|---|
| Summary Statistics | | | |
| $\bar{R}^2$ | 0.7423 | 0.7245 | 0.7377 |
| SEE | 2.5654 | 2.6522 | 2.5881 |
| F | 30.9300 | 28.3400 | 26.0528 |
| df | 6, 55 | 6, 55 | 7, 54 |
| DW | 1.5070 | 1.3987 | 1.5141 |
| Estimated Coefficients | | | |
| Constant | 12.5455 (4.3711) | −3.3579 (−1.9357) | 10.9164 (1.2446) |
| $\Delta P_t$ | 0.0287 (0.3309) | 0.0234 (0.2594) | 0.0328 (0.3643) |
| $\Delta W_t$ | 0.2551 (2.5422) | 0.2679 (2.5703) | 0.2523 (2.4667) |
| $U_t$ | −0.3214 (−2.8672) | −0.2304 (−2.1442) | −0.3229 (−2.8488) |
| $\Delta U_t$ | −0.0441 (−3.8284) | −0.0476 (−4.0396) | −0.0439 (−3.7778) |
| $D_{t-1}$ | −0.2097 (−3.9277) | | −0.1345 (−0.3482) |
| $(D_{t-1})^{-1}$ | | 256.6250 (3.2998) | |
| $(D_{t-1})^2$ | | | −0.0008 (−0.1968) |
| Dummy $C_t$ | 6.4157 (3.5468) | 4.8371 (1.9670) | 6.8500 (2.3917) |

NOTE: Figures in parentheses are estimated '$t$' values.

The impact of the compulsory arbitration system is also reflected by the estimated coefficient of $\Delta W_t$. Its magnitude is relatively small and indicates that, other things being equal, a 1 percentage point increase in the rate of change of money wages would lead to a 0.25 percentage point increase in $\Delta T$.

The coefficients of both the level and the rate of change of unemployment are significantly different from zero at significance levels of less than 1 per cent.[18] And an $F$ test indicates that the inclusion of these two variables in the equation significantly improves the fit.[19] The results indicate that, other things being equal, the partial effect of $U$ on $\Delta T$ is $-0.3$ while the partial effect of $\Delta U$ on $\Delta T$ is $-0.04$. In other words, if $U$ was 2 per cent and $\Delta U$ was zero, then, other things being equal, $\Delta T$ would be 0.6 percentage points lower than if there was no unemployment. And if $U$ was 2 per cent and $\Delta U$ was 1 per cent, then, other things being equal, $\Delta T$ would be $0.6 + 0.04 = 0.64$ percentage points lower.

The data fail to distinguish between the linear and non-linear forms of the density regressors. The three regressions produce comparable results except for the insignificance of the two density regressors in the quadratic form, which may be explained by multicollinearity.

As expected, the coefficient of $C$ is positive and highly significant. The results indicate that although a year within the period 1907–13 might have the same values for all explanatory variables as a year falling outside this period, $\Delta T$ would be 5 to 6 percentage points higher in the former instance than in the latter.

The model was tested to see if it is stable over the period of study. Following Sharpe's example, the overall period was split into two sub-periods, 1907–45 and 1946–69, and the Chow test was applied. It indicated that there was no change in the nature of the relationship between the two periods.[20] The model was also estimated for different periods and found to be insensitive to the addition of observations.[21] In addition, Regression 1 in Table 5.3 was estimated for the period 1907–65. The predicted values it produces for the period 1907–69 are plotted against the actual values of $\Delta T$ and are presented in Figure 5.2. The graph reveals that the model's predictive ability is satisfactory, and this is confirmed by Theil's Inequality Coefficient.

Finally, a hybrid equation containing all the variables used in the

18. Different lags on both $U$ and $\Delta U$ were allowed for, but their current values produced the most satisfactory results.
19. See Appendix B.6 for details of the test.
20. Given that the cost-of-living policy of the Commonwealth Court of Conciliation and Arbitration changed to some extent after 1953, it might be argued that a structural shift in the relationship occurred at this point. Unfortunately, the Chow test cannot be used to test this hypothesis because the period 1954–69 allows for insufficient degrees of freedom relative to the period 1907–53. However, in so far as the estimates for the two periods can be compared, they suggest that the relationship is not significantly different after 1953.
21. It was estimated for 1907–65, 1907–67, and 1907–69.

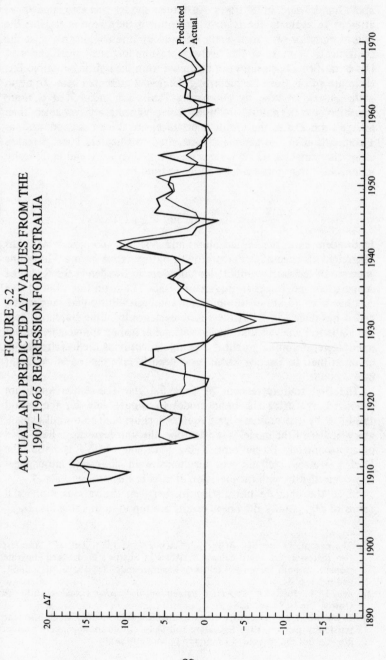

FIGURE 5.2
ACTUAL AND PREDICTED ΔT VALUES FROM THE
1907–1965 REGRESSION FOR AUSTRALIA

above model and in Sharpe's Australian model was estimated in an attempt to evaluate the relative strengths of the two models. But the hybrid equation was so severely affected by multicollinearity that the coefficients of most of the twelve regressors lost their significance.[22] Hence no firm conclusions can be drawn from the hybrid equation. But there are still reasons for preferring the model presented here. To begin with, as can be seen by comparing Tables 3.5 and 5.3, it is more parsimonious in nature: it uses fewer explanatory variables than Sharpe's model and the results it produces are at least as good. And, as a comparison of the arguments presented in Chapters 3 and 4 makes clear, the variables which it does use are theoretically and empirically more robust than those employed by Sharpe.

## Sweden

In Sweden, as in the United States and Australia, the government has attempted to encourage union growth by legislative means. The major example of legislative support for unionism in Sweden is the Rights of Association and Negotiation Act of 1936. The main intention of this Act has been to stimulate unionism amongst white-collar employees, and it has done so.[23] But there is no evidence from the graphs or from the statistical analysis that the legislation has had an appreciable impact upon aggregate union growth.[24] Hence, in applying the basic model of union growth to Sweden, there is no need to take the legislative factor into account.

The first four regressions in Table 5.4 give the results which are produced by fitting the basic model to annual data for the period 1914–70 by the ordinary least squares technique. The overall explanatory power of the model is satisfactory: the four regressions have a $\bar{R}^2$ of approximately 80 per cent, a low *SEE*, and a high *F* statistic. The Durbin–Watson statistic was inconclusive in all cases, although it improved slightly with the inclusion of $\Delta PS$ in Regressions 3 and 4.

Since the data do not distinguish between the various functional forms of $D_{t-1}$, only the linear results are reported in Table 5.4. $D_{t-1}$

22. The exceptions are $\Delta U$, $\Delta(W/P)_{t-1}$, $\Delta(W/P)_{t-2}$, $T/E^*$, and $\Delta E^*$. The last two regressors are the dominant variables in Sharpe's model, and they are suspect on both theoretical and empirical grounds. See above, pp. 50–51, and p. 53, n. 81.
23. See T. L. Johnston, *Collective Bargaining in Sweden* (London: Allen & Unwin, 1962), 94 and 124–37.
24. In the preliminary analysis, a dummy variable was introduced to allow for the possibility that the 1936 legislation had had a significant impact upon union growth. But the variable was found to be insignificant.

TABLE 5.4

THE DETERMINANTS OF THE RATE OF CHANGE OF UNION MEMBERSHIP IN SWEDEN, 1914–1970

| REGRESSION | 1<br>1914–1970 | 2<br>1914–1970 | 3<br>1914–1970 | 4<br>1914–1970 | 5<br>1914–1970 | 6<br>1914–1965 | 7<br>1914–1968 |
|---|---|---|---|---|---|---|---|
| **Summary Statistics** | | | | | | | |
| $\bar{R}^2$ | 0.7956 | 0.7916 | 0.8116 | 0.8088 | 0.8605 | 0.8216 | 0.8181 |
| SEE | 2.4150 | 2.4383 | 2.3186 | 2.3358 | 1.8741 | 2.3458 | 2.3148 |
| F | 73.9951 | 54.4413 | 61.5571 | 48.5767 | 67.8115 | 59.9761 | 61.9653 |
| df | 3, 52 | 4, 51 | 4, 51 | 5, 50 | 5, 48 | 4, 46 | 4, 49 |
| DW | 1.3700 | 1.3650 | 1.4971 | 1.4581 | 1.1795 | 1.6036 | 1.5527 |
| **Estimated Coefficients** | | | | | | | |
| Constant | 19.2051<br>(10.6816) | 19.2479<br>(10.2995) | 19.9337<br>(11.3620) | 20.1792<br>(11.0080) | 21.1714<br>(13.4518) | 20.6427<br>(11.3583) | 20.3324<br>(11.4557) |
| $\Delta P_t$ | 0.2445<br>(4.2210) | 0.2498<br>(3.1117) | 0.4194<br>(4.4851) | 0.4530<br>(3.9255) | 0.1295<br>(2.3052) | 0.4301<br>(4.5145) | 0.4219<br>(4.5095) |
| $\Delta w_t$ | | −0.0064<br>(−0.0964) | | −0.0325<br>(−0.5045) | | | |
| $U_t$ | −0.4627<br>(−5.4330) | −0.4648<br>(−5.2373) | −0.4312<br>(−5.2096) | −0.4408<br>(−5.1477) | −0.5045<br>(−7.2183) | −0.4353<br>(−5.1853) | −0.4363<br>(−5.2669) |
| $\Delta PS$ | | | −0.2464<br>(−2.3262) | −0.2558<br>(−2.3615) | | −0.2730<br>(−2.4857) | −0.2585<br>(−2.4183) |
| $D_{t-1}$ | −0.2393<br>(−10.2442) | −0.2394<br>(−10.1364) | −0.2524<br>(−10.9152) | −0.2535<br>(−10.8337) | −0.2450<br>(−11.5259) | −0.2690<br>(−10.7530) | −0.2608<br>(−10.9539) |
| $\Delta (w/P)_{t-1}$ | | | | | −0.1456<br>(−2.4495) | | |
| $\Delta (w/P)_{t-2}$ | | | | | −0.1753<br>(−2.5173) | | |

NOTE: Figures in parentheses are estimated 't' values.

has the expected sign and is highly significant. The magnitude of its estimated coefficient is just above 0.2 in all the regressions.

Unemployment is an important determinant of union growth in Sweden. Its estimated coefficient is highly significant,[25] and its magnitude suggests that if $U$ was 1 per cent, then, other things being equal, $\Delta T$ would be approximately 0.45 percentage points lower than it would be if unemployment was zero.

The estimated coefficient of $\Delta P_t$ is significantly different from zero and has the expected sign. Its magnitude in Regressions 1 and 2 suggests that, other things being equal, a 1 percentage point increase in $\Delta P$ would lead to a 0.25 percentage point increase in $\Delta T$. But Regressions 3 and 4 indicate that price rises do not have a constant effect upon union growth regardless of their size. The significance of $\Delta PS$ in these regressions indicates that price rises equal to or greater than 4 per cent will continue to cause $\Delta T$ to increase but at a lower rate.

In contrast to the price variable, the coefficient of $\Delta W_t$ has the wrong sign and is insignificant. A possible explanation for the insignificance of the wage variable is that multicollinearity is present in the model to a harmful degree. Such a conclusion is supported by the large magnitude of the correlation coefficient between $\Delta W_t$ and $\Delta P_t$ (0.82) and by the large drop which occurs in the overall $F$ statistic when $\Delta W_t$ is included in the equation. But the fact that the $\Delta P_t$ coefficient is insensitive to the inclusion or exclusion of the wage variable tends to contradict the multicollinearity argument.

In order to shed further light on the question of multicollinearity, a real wage variant of the basic model was employed. To begin with, $\Delta T$ was regressed on $\Delta(W/P)_t$, $U_t$, and $D_{t-1}$. The results revealed that $\Delta(W/P)_t$ is insignificant, and an $F$ test indicated that the constraint imposed by using this variable is invalid for Swedish data.[26] Lagged values of $\Delta(W/P)$ were then used on the assumption that the constraint may be valid in the long-run. These worked best when $\Delta P_t$ was also included in the equation, and the results are given in Regression 5 in Table 5.4.

The overall summary statistics indicate that 86 per cent of the variation in $\Delta T$ is explained by the regressors employed. The standard error of the estimate is low, and the large magnitude of the $F$ statistic indicates the overall significance of the regression. The Durbin–Watson statistic is still inconclusive; indeed, it is more unsatisfactory than in the case of the basic model. The signs, magnitudes, and significance of the unemployment and density coefficients are similar to those of their

---

25. The rate of change of unemployment was also employed as a regressor but its coefficient was insignificant, had the wrong sign, or possessed both faults.
26. See Appendix B.3 for details of the test.

counterparts in the basic model. Both $\Delta(W/P)_{t-1}$ and $\Delta(W/P)_{t-2}$ are significant, and their negative signs suggest that the lagged real wage variables represent a 'threat effect'. And the significant and positive coefficient of $\Delta P_t$ implies that current prices, representing the 'threat' and 'prosperity' effects, have an additional impact on $\Delta T$ over and above the impact of lagged prices which enters the equation as part of the real wage regressors.[27]

Unfortunately, the results of the real wage variant do not allow any firmer conclusions to be drawn about the multicollinearity problem. And taking these results in conjunction with those of the basic model, the only conclusion which can be drawn is that $\Delta W_t$ is insignificant and that its insignificance may be due either to multicollinearity or to the absence of the 'credit effect' for Sweden.

The model was tested to see if it is stable over the period of study. The way in which the bargaining system in Sweden has become more centralized since 1939 suggests that there may have been a change around this date in the structure of the relationship which the basic model describes.[28] Hence the overall period was broken into two sub-periods, 1914–38 and 1939–70, and the Chow test was applied. The test indicated that the basic model is not stable over time. In other words, the relationship before 1939 is significantly different from that after 1939.

Finally, in line with the analysis for other countries, the model was tested for its stability when additional observations were added and also for its predictive ability. Regressions 6 and 7 of Table 5.4 were estimated for the periods 1914–65 and 1914–68. A comparison of Regressions 3, 6, and 7 indicates that the model is insensitive to the addition of observations, and this is confirmed by the appropriate $F$ test. In addition, the predicted values produced for the period 1914–70 from Regression 6 are plotted against the actual values of $\Delta T$ in Figure 5.3. The predictions are reasonably satisfactory although poor for 1967–70. It is worth noting that the predictions are higher than the actuals for most of the period 1939–66, while they are lower than the actuals for most of the period 1928–39. Given that there is a structural break in the model around 1939, and given further the evidence about autocorrelated residuals, the less satisfactory nature of the predictions for Sweden as compared with those of other countries is not unexpected.

---

27. The significance of $\Delta P_t$ confirms that the effect of prices on $\Delta T$ is larger than that implied by the ratio, $\Delta(W/P)$. And, as argued above, p. 65, the omission of $\Delta P$ from the equation would involve a specification error which would affect the properties of the estimates.
28. See below, pp. 109–10.

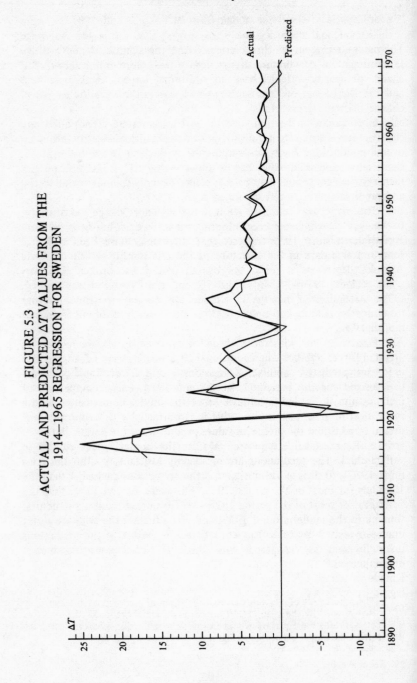

FIGURE 5.3
ACTUAL AND PREDICTED ΔT VALUES FROM THE
1914—1965 REGRESSION FOR SWEDEN

## Conclusion

The previous chapter specified and estimated a model of union growth. It employs the current rate of change of prices, the current rate of change of money wages, the lagged rate of change of unemployment, and the lagged level of union density as determinants of the rate of change of union membership. It also employs terms which allow the effects of prices and union density to be non-linear. The model is clearly satisfactory when judged in terms of the usual criterion of overall goodness of fit as well as in terms of the signs, magnitudes, and significance of the estimated regression coefficients. It is also satisfactory when judged in terms of its structural stability, data sensitivity, and predictive ability. But the chapter estimated the model for only a single country: the United Kingdom. In order to determine the extent to which the model's specification rests upon hypotheses which can be applied to other countries, the present chapter has taken the general form of the model and estimated it using data for the United States, Australia, and Sweden.

In applying the model to these countries, only one modification had to be made to its basic specification: allowance sometimes had to be made for the impact of government action upon union growth. This modification was not necessary for the United Kingdom or for Sweden. Although the Swedish government has passed legislation to encourage union growth, its main intention and effect have been to stimulate unionism among white-collar employees, and it does not appear to have had a significant impact upon the rate of change of aggregate union membership. In the United States, however, the government has had a most significant impact upon aggregate union growth, and hence a dummy variable had to be included in the model to allow for the government's influence between 1937 and 1947. Similarly, a dummy variable had to be included in the model for Australia to allow for the impact of government action upon union growth between 1907 and 1913.

Unemployment is a significant determinant of union growth in all four countries. In Australia both the level and the rate of change of unemployment affect union membership. In Sweden only the level of unemployment is significant, whereas only the rate of change of unemployment is significant in the United States. In the United Kingdom, unlike the other countries included in this study, there is a lagged relationship between the level of unemployment and union membership. And, as explained before, this implies that the rate of change of unemployment lagged one year is a significant determinant of union membership.[29]

29. See above, pp. 73–4.

The lagged level of union density is also a significant determinant of union membership in all four countries. But, once again, the form of the relationship varies between countries. The relationship is non-linear in the United States, whereas the linear and non-linear forms give equally good results for the other three countries included in the study.

The rate of change of prices is an important determinant of union growth in the United Kingdom, the United States, and Sweden. In the United Kingdom and Sweden the relationship is current and non-linear; in the United States it is lagged and linear. In Australia neither lagged nor unlagged price rises have a significant impact upon union growth.

The current rate of change of money wages is a significant determinant of union growth in the United Kingdom, the United States, and Australia. It is not significant in Sweden, although its lack of significance there may be due to multicollinearity.

Some of the basic results for the four countries are summarized in Table 5.5. They clearly vary in detail from one country to another, which is hardly surprising. The general form of the basic model leaves a number of specification questions to be determined empirically, and there is no reason to expect the data for the different countries to answer these questions in exactly the same way. Given that the answers differ, however, it is interesting to reflect on the reasons.

The insignificance of the price variable in Australia was expected and has already been commented upon. By tending to tie the basic wage to the retail price index, the arbitration system in Australia has largely protected the workers' pay from the eroding effects of inflation and thereby removed the threat which rising prices generally pose for workers' living standards. Not surprisingly, therefore, rising prices have not motivated Australian workers to unionize.

Workers in Sweden, the United Kingdom, and the United States have not generally had a national basic wage tied to the retail price index, and hence rising prices have threatened their living standards and thereby encouraged them to unionize. But price rises in the United States have not had an immediate impact upon union growth as they have in Sweden and the United Kingdom; their impact has occurred about a year later. This lag may be explained by differences between the industrial relations systems of these countries. As a reading of labour history quickly makes clear, employer hostility to unionism has generally been far more vigorous and virulent in the United States than in Sweden and the United Kingdom, and this has made it much more difficult for American unions to obtain recognition from employers. So has the way in which employers are organized for collective bargaining purposes in the United States. American unions have generally been forced to win recognition on a plant-by-plant basis by proving that they have majority representation in each plant. British and Swedish unions

# TABLE 5.5
## THE DETERMINANTS OF THE RATE OF CHANGE OF UNION MEMBERSHIP IN FOUR COUNTRIES

|  | United Kingdom 1893–1970 | United States 1897–1970 | Australia 1907–1969 | Sweden 1914–1970 |
|---|---|---|---|---|
| **Summary Statistics** | | | | |
| $\bar{R}^2$ | 0.7018 | 0.6860 | 0.7423 | 0.8088 |
| DW | 1.6352 | 1.4516 | 1.5200 | 1.4881 |
| **Estimated Coefficients** | | | | |
| $\Delta P_t$ | 0.5831 (5.8599) | | 0.0287 (0.3309) | 0.4530 (3.9255) |
| $\Delta P_{t-1}$ | | 0.5431 (3.6623) | | |
| $\Delta PS_t$ | −0.3861 (−2.6856) | | | −0.2558 (−2.3615) |
| $\Delta W_t$ | 0.4684 (4.1814) | 0.7053 (4.8528) | 0.2551 (2.5422) | −0.0325 (−0.5045) |
| $U_t$ | | | −0.3214 (−2.8672) | −0.4408 (−5.1477) |
| $\Delta U_t$ | | | −0.0441 (−3.8284) | |
| $U_{t-1}$ | −0.3506 (−1.3254) | | | |
| $U_{t-2}$ | 0.4028 (1.6119) | | | |
| $\Delta U_t^+$ | | −0.0775 (−2.2778) | | |
| $\Delta U_t^-$ | | 0.0727 (4.7907) | | |
| $D_{t-1}$ | −0.2029 (−5.4005) | | −0.2097 (−3.9277) | −0.2535 (−10.8337) |
| $(D_{t-1})^{-1}$ | | 122.3410 (9.3571) | | |
| Dummy $G_t$ | | 8.2208 (4.7534) | | |
| Dummy $C_t$ | | | 6.4157 (3.5468) | |

NOTE: Figures in parentheses are estimated '$t$' values.

have not generally had to prove majority representation, and they have generally been able to sign agreements with employers' associations which have had the effect of automatically transmitting union recognition throughout an entire industry.[30] In short, most British and Swedish industries have had a procedural framework within which unionism could increase more or less immediately in response to a stimulus such as the threat posed by rising prices. In contrast, the response provoked by such a stimulus in the United States is likely to be delayed by institutional roadblocks which have to be overcome before union membership can expand significantly.

There is another way in which the workers' response to price rises is different in the United States from that in Sweden and the United Kingdom. Price rises in the United States have a constant impact upon union growth regardless of their size. After price rises reach a level of about 4 per cent in Sweden and the United Kingdom, however, they have proportionately less impact upon union growth. The reason that British and Swedish workers are less sensitive than American workers to large price rises is that the former have more experience of them than the latter. The price series for the United States has a smaller mean and exhibits less variation than those for Sweden and the United Kingdom.[31] Indeed, the price series for the United States has only 12 out of 73 or 16 per cent of its observations which equal or exceed four percentage points; the corresponding figures are 21 out of 57 or 37 per cent for Sweden and 37 out of 77 or 48 per cent for the United Kingdom. Given these figures, it is hardly surprising that workers in Britain and Sweden are more blasé about rapid price inflation than those in the United States.

The differences in the exact way in which prices affect union growth in the different countries make a comparison of the magnitude of the price regression coefficients difficult.[32] But, so far as a comparison can

30. On this point see G. S. Bain, *The Growth of White-Collar Unionism* (Oxford: Clarendon Press, 1970), chap. 9; and Everett M. Kassalow, 'The Prospects for White-Collar Union Growth', *Industrial Relations*, V (October 1965), 41–2.
31. The mean of the rate of change of prices is 1.9 in the United States, 2.24 in the United Kingdom, and 2.87 in Sweden; its range of variation is 27 in the United States, 55 in the United Kingdom, and 53 in Sweden; and its standard deviation is 4.9 in the United States, 6.68 in the United Kingdom, and 7.45 in Sweden.
32. Although prices, wages, density, and unemployment were generally found to be significant determinants of union growth in the countries studied, the functional forms and lag structures of these variables varied from one country to another. This, together with the inadequacy of assuming that all the countries are from the same statistical population, makes it unjustifiable to pool the observations for all the countries together in a cross-section study. Strictly speaking, therefore, it is not valid to compare the magnitudes of the different coefficients across countries. But it was thought that a tentative comparison might be of interest.

be made, the results seem to suggest that prices have a smaller impact upon union growth in Sweden than in the United Kingdom and the United States. At least part of the explanation for this may be provided by the density of unionization. Sweden has generally had a higher level of union density than the other countries covered by this study; the average level of union density over the period studied is 50 per cent in Sweden, 43 per cent in Australia, 30 per cent in the United Kingdom, and 17 per cent in the United States. The higher the level of union density the less important the rate of change of prices is likely to be as a determinant of union growth. For its impact will be dampened on the upswing by the 'saturation effect' and on the downswing by the 'enforcement effect'. In other words, the 'saturation effect' will make it more difficult for an increase in the rate of change of prices to add to union membership because there are fewer workers left to recruit and they have less propensity and/or ability to unionize, whereas the 'enforcement effect' will make it more difficult for a decrease in the rate of change of prices to subtract from union membership because of the greater prevalence of social coercion and union security provisions.

A comparison of the magnitudes of the wage regression coefficients is complicated by the uncertainty over the significance of the results for Sweden. But even if the wage coefficient's lack of significance in Sweden is due to multicollinearity, there are reasons why the impact of wages upon union growth is likely to be smaller and less significant in Sweden than in the other countries covered by this study. To begin with, for the same reasons as applied in the case of the price variable, the higher the level of union density the less important the rate of change of wages is likely to be as a determinant of union growth. And, in so far as comparisons between the countries are possible, the results confirm this argument: the higher a country's average level of union density the smaller the magnitude of its wage coefficient.

Another reason the impact of wages upon union growth is likely to be smaller and less significant in Sweden than in the other countries covered by this study is provided by the system of collective bargaining. The more centralized it is the smaller the 'credit effect' is likely to be. For the more centralized the bargaining system the fewer the bargains, the more remote these will be from the workers, the less conscious they will be of the gains achieved, and hence the less likely these are to be credited to union activity. Conversely, the more decentralized the bargaining system the more conscious of wage rises workers are likely to be, and the more likely they are to link these rises with union activity.

The results for Sweden are consistent with such an argument. It has the lowest wage coefficient, and it has also had for many years the most centralized system of collective bargaining of all the countries included in this study. Before 1939 bargaining in Sweden occurred primarily at industry level. With the outbreak of the Second World War, LO and SAF, the major union and employer federations, began to engage in central negotiations at national level. In the immediate post-war years bargaining by individual unions was resumed, but it was guided by LO recommendations. And in the early 1950s central wage agreements once again began to be negotiated. In short, although some plant bargaining has occurred in Sweden over the years, it has generally been tightly constrained and regulated by industry-wide negotiations which, in turn, have tended to be guided by central negotiations at national level.[33]

The results for the other countries included in this study are also consistent with the argument that the more centralized the collective bargaining system the less important the rate of change of wages is likely to be as a determinant of union growth. The United States has the largest wage coefficient of all the countries covered by this study. It also has had the most decentralized bargaining system over the period as a whole. For it is predominantly a nation of small bargaining units which cover the employees of a single plant or a single employer.[34]

Since the end of the Second World War, collective bargaining in some industries in the United Kingdom has become even more decentralized than in the United States. But even today 'domestic' and 'workshop' bargaining affects probably only a minority of employees, and its incidence was considerably less before 1945. Industry-wide bargaining was the norm during the inter-war period, and before the First World War collective bargaining generally took place on a regional basis.[35] Hence the United Kingdom has generally had a more centralized bargaining system than the United States over the period as a whole, and the wage coefficient in the United Kingdom is smaller than that in the United States.

The bargaining system in Australia is more centralized than that in the United Kingdom. For almost 90 per cent of all Australian employees have their pay and conditions determined by 'awards' laid down by government tribunals. But the bargaining system is less centralized in Australia than in Sweden. For most Australian employees are covered by state awards; less than half of them are covered by

33. See *The Trade Union Situation in Sweden* (Geneva: International Labour Office, 1961), 58–62; Johnston, *op. cit.*, 279–91; and Steven D. Anderman, 'Central Wage Negotiation in Sweden: Recent Problems and Developments', *British Journal of Industrial Relations*, V (November 1967), 322–37.
34. About two-thirds of all collective agreements in the United States cover workers in a single plant. See Neil W. Chamberlain, *Labor* (New York: McGraw-Hill, 1958), 160–64.
35. See H. A. Clegg, *The System of Industrial Relations in Great Britain* (Oxford: Blackwell, 1972), chaps. 6 and 7.

national or federal awards.[36] Moreover, as Martin has pointed out, many of these awards

are not in fact the outcome of an arbitrator's decision, but of a prior agreement between unions and employers who have asked an arbitrator to convert their agreement into an award or determination . . . Even in the case of awards which are actually, as well as technically, the outcome of an arbitral decision, usually most of their clauses have been agreed on, leaving the arbitrator to decide only one or two disputed issues.[37]

And there are also 'over-award' payments which are generally negotiated at plant level. In short, collective bargaining in Australia is closely intertwined with compulsory arbitration, and the latter has tended to make the bargaining system there more centralized than in the United Kingdom but less centralized than in Sweden. In keeping with the intermediate position of the Australian bargaining system, the wage coefficient in Australia is smaller than in the United Kingdom but larger than in Sweden.

Although unemployment and the lagged level of union density have a significant impact upon union growth in all four countries, the way in which they affect the rate of change of union membership varies between countries. In the case of union density, the data fail to distinguish between the linear, quadratic, and inverse forms, except in the United States where they prefer the inverse. In the case of unemployment, it is sometimes the level, sometimes the rate of change, and sometimes both measures which affect union growth. The arguments put forward in Chapter 4 do not predict the exact way in which these variables enter the model,[38] and they offer no explanations for the different functional forms which have actually resulted from experimenting with the data.

But the arguments put forward in Chapter 4 may help to explain why there is a lag in the relationship between union growth and unemployment in the United Kingdom but not in the other countries covered by this study. In the case of the United Kingdom and the United States, at least part of the explanation may be provided by the different ways in which their membership series are compiled. The union membership series for the United States is derived mainly from

36. See K. F. Walker, *Australian Industrial Relations Systems, op. cit.*, 11, table 2.
37. Ross M. Martin, *Trade Unions in Australia* (Victoria: Penguin Books Australia, 1975), 25.
38. See pp. 65–70.

financial data on the subscription income of unions.[39] And hence if unemployed members fall into arrears, or even if union rules wholly or partially exempt them from paying subscriptions, their lapsed or special financial status will be reflected almost immediately in the union membership series. In contrast, the membership series for the United Kingdom is derived primarily from the membership records of individual unions, and, since most unions permit members to be in arrears for several months before removing their names from the records, unemployment will tend not to have an immediate impact upon the membership series.

Since the membership series of Australian and Sweden are derived in a similar way to that of the United Kingdom, there is no statistical reason for expecting a difference in behaviour between these countries. But the arguments advanced in Chapter 4 suggest other reasons which may explain why there is a delay in workers' reactions to unemployment in the United Kingdom and not in the other countries covered by this study. Perhaps the most obvious reason is the cost of union membership in the various countries. Even allowing for the fairly common union practice of waiving or at least reducing the subscriptions of unemployed workers, those in the United Kingdom will generally have found it less expensive to maintain their membership than those in other countries. For 'the bald truth of the matter', as Roberts has noted, 'is that British workers get their trade unionism on the cheap; in no other country in the world are union contributions, as a proportion of earnings, so low.'[40]

Unionists in the United Kingdom may have maintained their membership for longer periods when unemployed than those in other countries, not only because it has generally cost them less but also because they have generally valued it more. The decision to join a union is rarely a completely voluntary act, but it has probably been more often and more completely voluntary in the United Kingdom than in the other countries dealt with in this study. For compulsory unionism, as enforced by such union security provisions as the closed shop, the union shop, and preference clauses, has generally been much more common in Australia and the United States than in the United Kingdom.[41] Although formal union security provisions have been less

39. More specifically, the size of a union's membership is estimated by dividing its total annual subscription income by its average annual subscription rate. See Bain and Price, *op. cit.*
40. B. C. Roberts, *Trade Unions in a Free Society*, second edition (London: Hutchinson for the Institute of Economic Affairs, 1962), 91.
41. Approximately 40 per cent of union members in the United Kingdom were covered by union security provisions in the early 1960s. See W. E. J. McCarthy, *The Closed Shop in Britain* (Oxford: Blackwell, 1964),

common in Sweden than in the United Kingdom,[42] the density of unionization in Sweden has generally been very much higher than in the United Kingdom. The higher the level of union density the more likely it is that indifferent or unwilling employees will be socially coerced into becoming union members. Such employees are particularly likely to discontinue their membership if unemployed. In short, there is probably a larger proportion of unionists in Australia, Sweden, and the United States than in the United Kingdom who are likely to relinquish their union membership as soon as unemployment removes them from the scope of union security provisions or the social pressures of their workmates.

The differences in the exact way in which unemployment affects union growth in the different countries make a comparison of the magnitude of the unemployment regression coefficients very difficult. But, so far as a comparison can be made, the results seem to suggest that unemployment has a bigger impact upon union growth in Sweden and Australia than in the United Kingdom and the United States. The average level of union density in the period studied is also higher in Sweden and Australia (50 and 43 per cent respectively) than in the United Kingdom and the United States (30 and 17 per cent respectively). And, as in the case of the price and wage variables, the differences in the level of union density probably help to account for the differences in the size of the unemployment coefficients. Using the same logic as before, unemployment is likely to become a more important determinant of the rate of change of union membership the higher the density of unionization. For unemployment will weaken the 'saturation effect' on the upswing by effectively increasing the area for recruitment and it will lessen the scope of the 'enforcement effect' on the downswing by taking workers out of the labour market. To take the limiting case, if the density level were 100 per cent, the rate of change of union membership would be completely unaffected by an increase and little affected by a decrease in the rates of change of prices and wages. But it could still be affected by any change in the number of workers unemployed.

---

28. Approximately 80 per cent of the employees covered by collective agreements in the United States were employed under union security provisions in 1959. See Phelps, *op. cit.*, 259. There are no accurate figures for Australia, but it is well known that preference clauses and other forms of union security provisions are very common there not only in collective agreements but also in the awards made by arbitration tribunals. Indeed, there is survey evidence which indicates that a considerable proportion of Australian unionists have been compelled to become members and that they would resign their membership of they were able to. See Martin, *op. cit.*, 49–52.

42. See Johnston, *op. cit.*, 47–9.

The differences between the countries are in themselves interesting and reveal that as the industrial relations system varies from country to country so do the functional forms, lag structures, and coefficients of the variables included in the basic model. But these differences should not be allowed to detract from the fundamental similarity of the results. In general, the results for the United States, Australia, and Sweden are similar to those for the United Kingdom, and they confirm the argument that the rate of change of prices, the rate of change of wages, the level and/or rate of change of unemployment, and the lagged level of union density are significant determinants of the rate of change of union membership. And they also confirm that government action has had a significant impact upon union growth in Australia and the United States.

# 6
# Conclusions

The debate over the determinants of aggregate union growth has gone on for a long time. The early writers on the subject stressed the significance of the business cycle, although most of them were prepared to admit that other factors were also important. Later writers generally reversed the emphasis. Although they relied upon the explanatory power of the business cycle in certain historical contexts, they emphasized a number of secular forces and institutional factors. Indeed, some of them, such as Bernstein, went so far as to claim that the business cycle theory was 'without general validity'.

But the arguments of most of these writers were not well grounded empirically. And hence, although they assembled a lengthy list of possible determinants, their relationship to union growth was not firmly established. Recent writers have tried to remedy this deficiency by building econometric models of union growth which incorporate some of the factors mentioned by earlier writers. These models specify the variables more precisely and operationally, and thereby enable their relative importance to be more firmly established. But all these models possess theoretical, methodological, and statistical weaknesses which limit the confidence which can be placed in the results they produce.

This study has attempted to build a more satisfactory model of union growth. The general form of the model employs the rate of change of prices, the rate of change of wages, the level and/or rate of change of unemployment, and the level of union density as determinants of the rate of change of union membership. The functional forms and lag structures of these determinants as well as the magnitude of their impact upon union growth varied from one country to another. But only one modification had to be made to the model's basic specification: allowance had to be made in the United States and Australia for the impact of government action upon union growth. And when modified in this way, the model produced satisfactory results for all four countries.

But the model's satisfactory nature does not necessarily mean that it

115

is, to use Ashenfelter and Pencavel's words, 'an exact description of the historical progress of trade union membership'.[1] For all the data are subject to certain margins of error, and these limit the confidence that can be placed in the specific estimates produced by the model. Every attempt has been made, however, to obtain the best data available and considerable information on the sources, method of calculation, and reliability of the data is given in Appendix E and elsewhere.[2]

Regardless of how reliable the data may be, the model contains relatively few explanatory variables, and hence it might appear to be simplistic given the lengthy list of factors which previous writers have advanced as determinants of union growth. But there are several points to be borne in mind in this connection. First, the model is concerned with explaining aggregate rather than disaggregate patterns of union growth, and hence factors which are unique to particular industries, occupations, regions, or companies are likely to be irrelevant to the explanation.

Second, the model is concerned with explaining the rate of change as distinct from the level of union membership, and thus variables which are not volatile enough to cause changes in union membership at relatively short intervals are also irrelevant to the explanation. For example, such variables as the value system of the community, the extent of social mobility, and the industrial and occupational composition of the labour force are dominated by their time trends and consequently exhibit little annual variation.[3] Although their effect upon union growth would have to be allowed for in a level model by a time trend variable, there is no need to do this in a rate of change model because their impact is captured by the constant term of the equation.

Third, the model is not concerned with listing all the determinants of the rate of change of aggregate union membership but only with identifying those of a strategic nature. Hence it has omitted those variables which have a sporadic and unsystematic influence upon union growth. For 'to attempt to account for the unique or even the rare event', as Moore has noted, 'is to set an impossibly high standard for

1. Orley Ashenfelter and John H. Pencavel, 'American Trade Union Growth: 1900–1960', *Quarterly Journal of Economics*, LXXXIII (August 1969), 447.
2. See also G. S. Bain and R. J. Price, *Profiles of Union Growth* (Oxford: Blackwell, forthcoming); and G. S. Bain, R. Bacon, and J. Pimlott, 'The Labour Force', *Trends in British Society since 1900*, ed. A. H. Halsey (London: Macmillan, 1972), 97–128.
3. In the case of the occupational composition of the labour force, this point can be illustrated by examining the time series showing white-collar workers as a percentage of total employees which appears in G. S. Bain, *The Growth of White-Collar Unionism* (Oxford: Clarendon Press, 1970), 193.

theory.'[4] And it has not attempted to include such 'indirect and secondary' factors as union leadership whose impact upon union growth, as Chapter 2 has argued, is largely dependent upon and hence captured by the explanatory variables which are already included in the model.[5] For a multiplicity of determinants constitutes a threat to explanation and understanding. As Samuelson has noted,

Every theory, whether in the physical or biological or social sciences, distorts reality in that it oversimplifies. But if it is good theory, what is omitted is outweighed by the beam of illumination and understanding that is thrown over the diverse empirical data.[6]

Another charge which might be levelled against the model is that of simultaneity. Hines has argued that union density is a rough quantitative index of union power or 'pushfulness'.[7] And since union membership is an important component of union density, it might be argued that the direction of causation flows from $\Delta T$ to $\Delta W$ and through it to $\Delta P$ instead of or as well as from $\Delta W$ and $\Delta P$ to $\Delta T$. But such a causal relationship is improbable. For, as several writers have argued at length, there are a number of practical, theoretical, methodological, and empirical reasons why neither union membership nor the union density of which it is a component make an adequate index of union power.[8]

Even if there were a simultaneous relationship between $\Delta T$, $\Delta W$, and $\Delta P$, the ordinary least squares estimates given in this study would still be acceptable. For there are good reasons for estimating a simultaneous equation system by ordinary least squares techniques rather than by

4. W. E. Moore, 'Notes for a General Theory of Labor Organization', *Industrial and Labor Relations Review*, XIII (April 1960), 387.
5. See pp. 22–3.
6. Paul A. Samuelson, *Economics: An Introductory Analysis*, sixth edition (New York: McGraw-Hill, 1964), 10.
7. See A. G. Hines, 'Trade Unions and Wage Inflation in the United Kingdom, 1893–1961', *Review of Economic Studies*, XXXI (October 1964), 221–52; and *idem*, 'Wage Inflation in the United Kingdom, 1948–62: A Disaggregated Study', *Economic Journal*, LXXIX (March 1969), 66–89.
8. See D. L. Purdy and G. Zis, 'Trade Unions and Wage Inflation in the UK: A Reappraisal', *Essays in Modern Economics*, ed. Michael Parkin and A. R. Nobay (London: Longman, 1973), 294–327; *idem*, 'On the Concept and Measurement of Trade Union Militancy', *Inflation and Labour Markets*, ed. D. Laidler and D. Purdy (Manchester: Manchester University Press, 1974), 38–60; R. Ward and G. Zis, 'Trade Union Militancy as an Explanation of Inflation: An International Comparison', *Manchester School of Economics and Social Studies*, XLII (March 1974), 46–56. See also Bain and Price, *op. cit.*

such simultaneous techniques as two-stage least squares.[9] Hence while building simultaneous equation systems would allow for any interrelationship which might exist between $\Delta T$, $\Delta W$, and $\Delta P$ in the various countries covered by this study, it would shed little additional light on the process of union growth. For since such systems may still be estimated by the ordinary least squares technique, their unionization equations would be identical in all respects to those which have been estimated here.

A final objection which might be raised against the model concerns the time period which it covers. It has been estimated from data which apply primarily to the twentieth century, and hence the model might be held not to apply to earlier periods of union growth. The precise details of the model and the estimates it produces probably do not apply to earlier periods of union growth, but the broad relationship which it describes almost certainly does. The Wisconsin School has presented evidence, albeit partial and imperfect, which supports this contention for the United States in the nineteenth century.[10] So has Ulman who has demonstrated that the formation of new unions in the United States after 1863 was highly sensitive to the business cycle.[11] And Hobsbawm has gleaned evidence from a variety of European countries which indicates that there has been a broad if imprecise relationship between economic fluctuations and various social move-

9. The choice of the estimation technique for a simultaneous equation system is not clear cut as there is a trade-off between the advantages of the various techniques. For example, although ordinary least squares estimates are biased and inconsistent, they have smaller variance around their biased means than the biased and consistent estimates obtained by other methods such as two-stage least squares. See J. Johnston, *Econometric Methods*, second edition (New York: McGraw-Hill, 1972), 408–18. In addition, two-stage least squares and other simultaneous techniques are more sensitive to multicollinearity than are ordinary least squares estimates. See L. R. Klein and M. Nakamura, 'Singularity in the Equation Systems of Econometrics: Some Aspects of the Problem of Multicollinearity', *International Economic Review*, III (September 1962), 274–99; and L. R. Klein, *A Textbook of Econometrics*, second edition (Englewood Cliffs, N.J.: Prentice Hall, 1974), 188–95. For further points see the papers by Hildreth, Klein, and Liu in *Econometrica*, XXVIII (October 1960), 846–71; and J. S. Cramer, *Empirical Econometrics* (Amsterdam: North-Holland, 1969), 131–4. After reviewing all the arguments, Theil concludes that 'although the method of ordinary least squares can no longer claim to have the brilliant properties which earlier econometricians thought it had, it can be regarded as one of the few one-eyed men who are eligible for king in the country of the blind.' See H. Theil, *Economic Forecasts and Policy*, second edition (Amsterdam: North-Holland, 1961), 239.
10. See above, pp. 5–6.
11. Lloyd Ulman, *The Rise of the National Trade Union* (Cambridge, Mass.: Harvard University Press, 1955), 3–7.

ments such as unionism since 1800.[12] Indeed, there is some evidence from these studies that the impact of the business cycle upon union growth may have been even stronger in the nineteenth century than during more recent times. Be that as it may, the great bulk of union growth has taken place during the twentieth century, and the business cycle has certainly had a significant impact upon it during this period.

12. E. J. Hobsbawm, 'Economic Fluctuations and Some Social Movements since 1800', *Economic History Review*, V, no. 1 (1952), 1–25.

# A Note on the Regression Technique Used in this Study

## Method of Estimation

The method of estimation used in this study is the ordinary least squares technique. The method and its properties are well known. Briefly, the method supposes that the dependent variable observations are generated as a linear combination of the explanatory variable observations and an additive error term. In other words, $Y = \alpha + \beta X + \epsilon$, where $Y$ is the dependent variable, $X$ is the explanatory variable, $\epsilon$ is the error term, and $\alpha$ and $\beta$ are the unknown parameters to be estimated. Given the observations on the different variables, the method estimates the unknown parameters in such a way as to minimize the sum of the squared deviations from the line determining the dependent variable observations.

This may be illustrated graphically as follows:

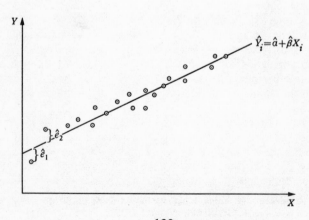

The circled dots are the $Y$ observations, the line represents the regression line $\hat{\alpha} + \beta X_i$, and $\hat{e}_i$ is the deviation of the $i$th observation of $Y$ from the value predicted by the line for $Y_i$. That is, $\hat{e}_i$ equals $Y_i - \hat{Y}_i$. The method of estimation minimizes the sum of squares of these deviations; that is, it finds the values of $\hat{\alpha}$ and $\hat{\beta}$ that minimize $\Sigma \hat{e}_i^2$.

The ordinary least squares method makes a number of assumptions:

(a) The error term $\epsilon$ for each observation is on average zero; that is, $E(\epsilon_i) = 0$ for each observation $(i = 1, \ldots n)$.

(b) The error terms in different observations are independent of each other, and their variances are the same for all observations.

(c) The explanatory variables are random variables that are distributed independently from the error term.

(d) There are at least as many observations as there are parameters to be estimated, and there is no exact linear relationship between the explanatory variables. In other words, if $X_1$ and $X_2$ are two explanatory variables determining $Y$, then it is assumed that there does not exist a relation between them such as, for example, $X_1 = aX_2$ where $a$ is constant. If such a relationship does exist, the estimating procedure breaks down. Such relations are rare in practice, and there exist instead approximate relationships which result in high correlations between $X_1$ and $X_2$.

On the basis of these assumptions, the resulting least squares estimates possess several desired properties.

### Desired Properties of the Estimates

To understand the properties, it is important to remember that the estimates are obtained from a given set of data while the unknown parameters refer to 'true' or 'population' parameters. Thus the estimates will not be an exact measure of the true parameters except by chance. In short, the mere fact of working with sample observations rather than population values implies a difference between the estimate $\hat{\beta}$ and the true parameter $\beta$. This is called the sampling error, $\hat{\beta} - \beta$, and it differs from sample to sample since each sample will give a different estimate of $\hat{\beta}$.

Given the different estimates of $\hat{\beta}$, the question arises whether these differences result primarily from sampling errors. In other words, if all the possible samples were available, would they give on average the true parameters? And if the sample size was to increase indefinitely approaching the population, would that difference disappear in the limit? The answers to these questions determine the desired properties.

These are:

(a) *Unbiasedness*
The estimate of $\hat{\beta}$ is an unbiased estimate of $\beta$ if the former's expected value is equal to the true parameter $\beta$. In other words, if all the possible samples were available and different estimates were obtained from these samples (say $\hat{\beta}_1, \hat{\beta}_2, \ldots$) then the average estimate $E(\hat{\beta}) = \beta$. If this is not the case, then the difference is called the bias; that is,

$$|E(\hat{\beta}) - \beta| = \text{Bias}$$

(b) *Efficiency*
Different methods of estimation give different estimates with different variances. The estimates with the smallest variances as compared with those obtained from other estimating techniques are the efficient estimates.

(c) *Best Linear Unbiased Estimates*
Under the above assumptions, the ordinary least squares estimates are unbiased, have the smallest variance compared with all other unbiased estimators (that is, they are efficient), and are linear functions of the sample observations. They are known as the best linear unbiased estimates or BLUE.

(d) *Asymptotic Unbiasedness and Consistency*
An estimate $\hat{\beta}$ is asymptotically unbiased if the bias approaches zero as the sample size approaches infinity. If its variance also approaches zero in the limit, then the estimate is consistent.

(e) *Asymptotic Efficiency*
The asymptotically efficient estimators are those consistent estimators whose variance approaches zero the fastest.

## Problems Affecting the Desired Properties of the Estimate
The ordinary least squares estimates are BLUE under the assumptions stated above. But some of these assumptions may not hold in practice, and it is important to see how their violation affects the properties of the estimates.

(a) *Unbiasedness*
The critical assumption for the ordinary least squares estimates to be unbiased is that the explanatory variables are independently distributed from the error term. If this assumption is violated, then the estimates will be biased and, in general, inconsistent. The

situations which lead to the violation of this assumption are:
(i) the omission of a relevant explanatory variable;
(ii) the misspecification of the functional form;
(iii) errors of measurement in the explanatory variables;
(iv) feedback between the dependent and explanatory variables; and
(v) the inclusion of the lagged dependent variable as an explanatory variable.

(b) *Efficiency*
The critical assumption for the ordinary least squares estimates to be efficient is that the error terms in different observations are independent of each other and have the same variances for all observations. If the error terms in the different observations are related to each other, then they are said to be *autocorrelated.*

Autocorrelation may arise as a result of:
(i) errors of measurement in the dependent variable;
(ii) omission of serially correlated explanatory variables where the serial correlation in the omitted variables is pervasive and the omitted variables tend to move in phase; and
(iii) misspecification of the functional form of the relationship between variables (for example, fitting a linear instead of a quadratic which is a special case in (ii) above).

The consequences of autocorrelation are:
(i) unbiased but inefficient estimates;
(ii) the variance formula underestimates the true variance, and hence the $t$- and $F$-statistics are not strictly valid; and
(iii) inefficient prediction.

**Multicollinearity**
A multicollinearity problem arises if two or more of the explanatory variables are so highly correlated that it becomes difficult to disentangle their separate effects upon the dependent variable. The multicollinearity problem is one of degree. If there is an exact linear relationship between two or more variables (perfect correlation), then the estimating procedure breaks down. Fortunately, the relationship is generally not exact, and it is generally possible to obtain the estimates. The estimates possess all the desired properties but they are imprecise; that is, they have unduly large standard errors. If there is a severe multicollinearity problem, the estimates will be in an unduly wide range and in some situations a coefficient may appear insignificant when it is in fact significant. In short, if multicollinearity is present in serious degree, it is difficult to draw any conclusions about the magnitude and significance of the coefficients.

**Summary Statistics**

(a) $R^2$ *and* $\bar{R}^2$

The $R^2$ is a summary statistic which measures the goodness of the fit. It indicates the percentage of variation in the dependent variable that is explained by the variations in the explanatory variables. An $R^2$ of 0.9, for example, implies that 90 per cent of the variation in $Y$ is explained by the variation in $X$.

$$R^2 = \frac{\text{Explained Sum of Squares}}{\text{Total Sum of Squares}}$$

or

$$= 1 - \frac{\text{Unexplained Sum of Squares}}{\text{Total Sum of Squares}}$$

Some models use more explanatory variables than others, and hence have fewer degrees of freedom. (The number of degrees of freedom equals the number of observations minus the number of estimated parameters.) To allow the explanatory power of models containing different numbers of explanatory variables to be compared, an alternative measure of the goodness of fit is generally used. It is the corrected $R^2$.

$$\bar{R}^2 = 1 - \frac{\text{Unexplained Sum of Squares}}{\text{Total Sum of Squares}} \frac{n-1}{n-k}$$

where $n$ is the number of observations and $k$ is the number of parameters estimated.

(b) *Standard Error of the Estimated Regression*

The variance of the estimated regression is the ratio of the unexplained sum of squares to the number of degrees of freedom available. It is the mean of the unexplained sum of squares. The *SEE* is the square root of that variance. It is given by the formula:

$$SEE = \sqrt{\frac{\text{Unexplained Sum of Squares}}{n-k}}$$

where $n$ is the number of observations and $k$ is the number of parameters estimated. The smaller the *SEE* the better the fit of the equation.

(c) *F-statistic*

The $F$-statistic measures the overall significance of the regression. It is described in detail in Appendix B.2.

## (d) *Durbin–Watson Statistic*

The DW statistic tests for the existence of positive autocorrelation. It is defined as:

$$DW = \frac{\sum\limits_{t-i}^{n} (\hat{e}_t - \hat{e}_{t-1})^2}{\sum\limits_{t=1}^{n} \hat{e}_t^2}$$

where $\hat{e}_t$ is the value of the $t$-th residual. Having calculated the above statistic, it is compared to the bounds given by Durbin and Watson in most econometric textbooks. If the calculated DW is below the lower bound, it is indicative of positive autocorrelation. If the calculated DW is greater than the upper bound, then there is no evidence of positive autocorrelation. If the calculated DW is greater than the lower limit but smaller than the upper limit, then the test is inconclusive. The test may also be used for negative autocorrelation by subtracting the calculated DW from 4 and applying the same procedure.

## Appendix B

# Statistical Testing

## B.1 Testing the Significance of Individual Regression Coefficients

The '$t$' test was used to test the adequacy of the estimated regression coefficients of individual variables. Assuming the aim is to test the hypothesis that in the relationship, $Y = \alpha + \beta X + \epsilon$, $\beta = 0$, against the alternative hypothesis that $\beta \neq 0$, the steps in the procedure are as follows:

(a) Calculate the standard error of $\hat{\beta}$.

(b) Calculate $t_{observed} = \hat{\beta}/SE(\hat{\beta})$.

(c) Compare the calculated $t$, at the chosen significance level and the appropriate number of degrees of freedom, with the tabulated $t$ given in any statistics textbook.

(d) If $t_{observed} < t_{tabular}$, then accept the null hypothesis that $\beta$ is not significantly different from zero. If $t_{observed} \geqslant t_{tabular}$, then reject the null hypothesis and accept the alternative hypothesis that $\beta$ is significantly different from zero.

(e) A rough rule of thumb is that the regression coefficient is significantly different from zero if $t \geqslant 2$.

## B.2 Testing the Overall Significance of a Regression

An $F$-statistic together with the degrees of freedom are given for each regression reported in the monograph. These computed $F$ values should be compared with the tabulated values (or theoretical $F$ values given in many statistics and econometrics textbooks) with the appropriate degrees of freedom. If the computed $F$ is greater than the tabular $F$ at a given significance level, then the overall significance of the regression is accepted; in other words, the null hypothesis that all the regressors employed have no influence on the dependent variable is rejected. If the computed $F$ is smaller than the tabular $F$ at a given significance level, then the null hypothesis is accepted at that significance level.

In technical terms, the aim is to test the null hypothesis that

$$H_0 : \beta_1 = \beta_2 = \beta_3 = \ldots = \beta_k = 0$$

against the alternative hypothesis that

$$H_1 : \beta_1 \neq \beta_2 \neq \beta_3 \neq \ldots \neq \beta_k = 0$$

where the $\beta_i$s are the regression coefficients of the $k$ regressors. Compare the computed $F$ with the theoretical $F$ at a given level of significance; if the former is greater than the latter, the null hypothesis is rejected in favour of the alternative hypothesis.

In general, high values of the computed $F$ suggest a significant relationship between the dependent variable and the employed regressors.

### .3 Testing a Restriction Imposed on the Relationship between Two or More Variables
The procedure has five steps:

(a) Fit the *unrestricted* form of the relationship, and obtain its sum of squares of residuals (or unexplained sum of squares), say,

$$\Sigma e_1^2.$$

(b) Fit the *restricted* form of the relationship, and obtain its unexplained sum of squares, say,

$$\Sigma e_2^2.$$

(c) Compute

$$F_{\text{observed}} = \frac{\Sigma e_2^2 - \Sigma e_1^2}{\Sigma e_1^2} (N - k)$$

where $N$ is the number of observations and $k$ is the number of estimated parameters including the constant.

(d) Obtain at a given significance level (5 or 1 per cent) from the $F$ tables the value of $F$ associated with 1 degree of freedom (assuming *one* restriction) for the numerator and $N - k$ degrees of freedom for the denominator.

(e) Compare $F_{\text{observed}}$ and $F_{\text{tabular}}$. If $F_{\text{observed}} > F_{\text{tabular}}$ at the chosen level of significance, then reject the restriction at the chosen level of significance. If $F_{\text{observed}} < F_{\text{tabular}}$, then accept the restriction at this level of significance.

## B.4 Testing the Equality between Two Sets of Coefficients in Two Linear Regressions

This test is referred to in the text as the Chow test and it is used to assess the structural stability of the model. The procedure of the test is to divide the period of estimation into two sub-periods at the point where the structural shift is suspected. The relationship is estimated separately for the two sub-periods as well as for the overall period. Denote the sums of squares of residuals from each regression as:

$Q_1$ is the sum of squares of residuals from sub-period 1;
$Q_2$ is the sum of squares of residuals from sub-period 2; and
$Q_p$ is the sum of squares of residuals from the pooled or overall period.

The computed $F$ is then calculated as follows:

$$F_{computed} = \frac{[Q_p - (Q_1 + Q_2)]/k}{(Q_1 + Q_2)/N - 2k}$$

where $N$ is the number of observations and $k$ is the number of estimated parameters including the constant term.

Finally, the theoretical $F$ is obtained from the $F$-table at the chosen significance level, with $(k, N - 2k)$ degrees of freedom. The computed $F$ and the tabular $F$ are then compared; and if the computed $F$ is found to be larger than the tabular $F$, then the hypothesis that the two sub-periods differ significantly is accepted. In other words, the test would indicate that the model is not stable over time or that a structural shift took place at the break point. But if the computed $F$ is smaller than the tabular $F$ at the chosen significance level, then the alternative hypothesis that the two periods do not differ significantly is accepted.

## B.5 Testing the Stability of Regression Coefficients when Increasing the Sample Size

This procedure has sometimes been referred to in the text as testing the model's data sensitivity. The aim of the test is to investigate the stability of the estimated coefficient when the sample size increases. If the additional observations are more numerous than the number of parameters in the function, then the Chow test described above may be used; that is, the additional observations may be used as if they were a separate sample.

But if the additional observations are fewer than the number of parameters, then the procedure is as follows:

(a) Obtain the sum of squares of the residuals from the original sample $(\Sigma e_0^2)$ of size $n_1$ observations.

(b) Obtain the sum of squares of the residuals from the enlarged sample size of $n_1 + n_2$ where $n_2$ is the number of additional observations. Denote that sum as $\Sigma e_L^2$.

(c) Compute the $F$ ratio as

$$F_{computed} = \frac{(\Sigma e_L^2 - \Sigma e_0^2)/n_2}{\Sigma e_L^2/n_1 - k}$$

where $k$ is defined as before.

(d) Obtain the theoretical $F$ at a given level of significance with $(n_2, n_1 - k)$ degrees of freedom and compare the two ratios.

(e) If the computed $F$ is greater than the tabular $F$, accept that the structural coefficients are unstable; in other words, they are sensitive to additional observations and change as the sample size increases. If the computed $F$ is less than the tabular $F$, then the coefficients are stable.

## .6 Testing the Improvement in Fit from Additional Explanatory Variables

Another use of the $F$-statistic is to test the hypothesis that an additional explanatory variable(s) adds significantly to the explanation of the variation in the dependent variable. The procedure is as follows:

(a) From the regression employing only $m$ explanatory variables (including the constant term) and the regression employing $k$ ($>m$) explanatory variables, obtain the following:

$\Sigma \hat{y}_1^2$, the explained sum of squares from the regression with $m$ explanatory variables;

$\Sigma \hat{y}_2^2$, the explained sum of squares from the regression with $k$ explanatory variables; and

$\Sigma e_2^2$, the sum of squares of residuals from the regression employing $k$ explanatory variables.

(b) Define

$$F_{computed} = \frac{(\Sigma \hat{y}_2^2 - \Sigma \hat{y}_1^2)/k - m}{\Sigma e_2^2/N - k}$$

where $N$ is the number of observations, and $k$ and $m$ are the number of estimated parameters in the different regressions (including the constant term).

(c) Compare the computed $F$ with the tabular $F$ obtained from tables with $(k - m, N - k)$ degrees of freedom at the chosen significance level. If the computed $F$ is greater than the tabular $F$, conclude that the additional variable(s) improves the fit significantly. If the computed $F$ is less than the tabular $F$, conclude that the additional variable(s) does not improve the fit significantly.

129

# Appendix C

# Theil's Inequality Coefficient

Theil's inequality coefficient ($U$) was used as a measure of the predictive accuracy of the model. This coefficient is given by the formula:

$$U = \frac{\sqrt{\dfrac{1}{n} \Sigma (P_t - A_t)^2}}{\sqrt{\dfrac{1}{n} \Sigma A_t^2}}$$

where $P$ represents the predicted values, $A$ the actual values, and $n$ the number of predictions made. In other words, $U$ is the standardized root mean square error. In the case of perfect forecasting, $U = 0$; that is, every predicted value is equal to the actual value, and hence $P_t = A_t$ for all $t$, and the numerator is zero. As forecasting accuracy deteriorates, $U$ rises and has no upper bound. If a forecaster predicts no change throughout the whole period (that is, $P_t = 0$ for all $t$), then $U = 1$ and clearly an inequality coefficient approaching this unitary magnitude indicates that the forecasts are poor.

Since forecasting errors may arise in different ways, Theil decomposes the mean square error into three terms. Each relates to a different type of prediction error, and he derives three inequality proportions defined as:

$$U^M = \frac{(\bar{P} - \bar{A})^2}{\dfrac{1}{n} \Sigma (P_t - A_t)^2}$$

$$U^S = \frac{(S_P - S_A)^2}{\dfrac{1}{n} \Sigma (P_t - A_t)^2}$$

$$U^C = \frac{2(1-r)S_P S_A}{\frac{1}{n}\Sigma(P_t - A_t)^2}$$

where $\bar{P}$ is the mean of the predicted values, $\bar{A}$ is the mean of the actual values, $S_P$ is the standard deviation of the predicted values, $S_A$ is the standard deviation of the actual values, $r$ is the correlation coefficient between the predicted and actual values, and $U^M + U^S + U^C = 1$. The first proportion, $U^M$, is known as the bias proportion of forecasting error, and results from underprediction or overprediction of the average change. The second proportion, $U^S$, is known as the variance proportion of the mean square error, and results from underprediction or overprediction of the variance of the changes. Finally, $U^C$, known as the covariance proportion, is the proportion of forecasting error that is random. If forecasts cannot be perfect, it is desirable that they should at least be free of systematic errors; and hence both $U^M$ and $U^S$ should be small, leaving the forecasting errors to be predominantly of the random or unsystematic type, $U^C$. In short, good forecasters should be able to remove systematic errors.

# Correlation Coefficients

The following tables give the simple correlation coefficients between the different regressors employed in the reported regressions.

TABLE D.1
UNITED KINGDOM, 1893–1970

|  | $\Delta P_t$ | $U_{t-1}$ | $U_{t-2}$ | $\Delta PS_t$ | $\Delta W_t$ |
|---|---|---|---|---|---|
| $U_{t-1}$ | -0.3109 | | | | |
| $U_{t-2}$ | -0.2166 | 0.9232 | | | |
| $\Delta PS_t$ | 0.7079 | -0.2836 | -0.2597 | | |
| $\Delta W_t$ | 0.6663 | -0.4631 | -0.2832 | 0.6217 | |
| $\Delta P_{t-1}$ | 0.2952 | -0.4935 | -0.2759 | 0.4123 | 0.7773 |
| $D_{t-1}$ | 0.1197 | -0.3136 | -0.3301 | 0.1861 | 0.3060 |
| $(D_{t-1})^2$ | 0.1060 | -0.3990 | -0.4153 | 0.1571 | 0.3101 |
| $(D_{t-1})^{-1}$ | -0.1425 | 0.0992 | 0.1157 | -0.2335 | -0.2700 |

Other correlations which do not appear in this table are those between $D_{t-1}$ and $(D_{t-1})^2$ (0.9880) and between $D_{t-1}$ and $\Delta P_{t-1}$ (0.2420).

TABLE D.2
UNITED STATES, 1897–1970

|  | $\Delta W_t$ | $\Delta P_{t-1}$ | $\Delta U_t^+$ | $\Delta U_t^-$ | Dummy $G_t$ | $D_{t-1}$ |
|---|---|---|---|---|---|---|
| $\Delta P_{t-1}$ | 0.4537 | | | | | |
| $\Delta U_t^+$ | -0.3379 | 0.1391 | | | | |
| $\Delta U_t^-$ | -0.3937 | -0.0388 | 0.3506 | | | |
| Dummy $G_t$ | 0.2291 | 0.1017 | -0.0450 | -0.1126 | | |
| $D_{t-1}$ | 0.1390 | 0.2412 | -0.0587 | 0.1679 | 0.1492 | |
| $(D_{t-1})^2$ | 0.1312 | 0.2175 | -0.0651 | 0.1911 | 0.1058 | 0.9908 |
| $(D_{t-1})^{-1}$ | -0.1088 | -0.2503 | -0.0337 | -0.1339 | -0.2055 | |

## Correlation Coefficients

### TABLE D.3
### AUSTRALIA, 1907–1969

|  | $\Delta P_t$ | $\Delta W_t$ | $U_t$ | $\Delta U_t$ | $C_t$ | $D_{t-1}$ |
|---|---|---|---|---|---|---|
| $\Delta W_t$ | 0.6571 |  |  |  |  |  |
| $U_t$ | −0.4864 | −0.5757 |  |  |  |  |
| $\Delta U_t$ | −0.1950 | −0.1240 | 0.1493 |  |  |  |
| Dummy $C_t$ | 0.0289 | −0.0462 | −0.0999 | 0.0291 |  |  |
| $(D_{t-1})^{-1}$ | −0.0250 | −0.1825 | 0.1421 | −0.0006 | 0.8529 |  |
| $D_{t-1}$ | 0.1035 | 0.2646 | −0.3336 | 0.0286 | −0.6984 |  |
| $(D_{t-1})^2$ | 0.1401 | 0.2903 | −0.3995 | 0.0375 | −0.5945 | 0.9869 |

### TABLE D.4
### SWEDEN, 1914–1970

|  | $\Delta P_t$ | $U_t$ | $D_{t-1}$ | $\Delta PS_t$ |
|---|---|---|---|---|
| $U_t$ | −0.5224 |  |  |  |
| $D_{t-1}$ | 0.0073 | −0.6256 |  |  |
| $\Delta PS_t$ | 0.8213 | −0.2136 | −0.2635 |  |
| $\Delta W_t$ | 0.8166 | −0.5746 | 0.1120 | 0.5838 |

Additional correlations involving the lagged $\Delta(W/P)$ variable were

|  | $\Delta(W/P)_{t-1}$ | $\Delta(W/P)_{t-2}$ |
|---|---|---|
| $\Delta(W/P)_{t-2}$ | 0.4569 |  |
| $U_t$ | 0.0758 | 0.1953 |
| $D_{t-1}$ | 0.1235 | 0.1775 |

Other correlations involving $(D_{t-1})^2$ and $(D_{t-1})^{-1}$ are not given since the results were discussed in terms of the linear form of density.

# Statistical Sources

TABLE E.1
THE BASIC DATA FOR THE UNITED KINGDOM

| Year | Total Union Membership (000s) | Potential Union Membership (000s) | Retail Prices (1930 = 100) | Wage Earnings (1930 = 100) | Unemployment (%) |
|---|---|---|---|---|---|
| 1892 | 1,576 | 14,803 | 57.5 | 43.0 | 6.3 |
| 93 | 1,559 | 14,947 | 57.0 | 43.0 | 7.5 |
| 94 | 1,530 | 15,092 | 54.2 | 43.0 | 6.9 |
| 95 | 1,504 | 15,236 | 53.1 | 43.0 | 5.8 |
| 96 | 1,608 | 15,370 | 53.1 | 43.0 | 3.3 |
| 97 | 1,731 | 15,524 | 54.2 | 44.0 | 3.3 |
| 98 | 1,752 | 15,668 | 55.8 | 45.0 | 2.8 |
| 99 | 1,911 | 15,812 | 54.7 | 46.0 | 2.0 |
| 1900 | 2,022 | 15,957 | 58.1 | 49.0 | 2.5 |
| 1 | 2,025 | 16,101 | 57.6 | 49.0 | 3.3 |
| 2 | 2,013 | 16,267 | 57.6 | 48.0 | 4.0 |
| 3 | 1,994 | 16,433 | 58.1 | 48.0 | 4.7 |
| 4 | 1,967 | 16,599 | 58.7 | 46.0 | 6.0 |
| 5 | 1,997 | 16,765 | 58.7 | 46.0 | 5.0 |
| 6 | 2,210 | 16,932 | 59.2 | 48.0 | 3.6 |
| 7 | 2,513 | 17,098 | 60.9 | 50.0 | 3.7 |
| 8 | 2,485 | 17,264 | 59.2 | 49.0 | 7.8 |
| 9 | 2,477 | 17,430 | 59.8 | 49.0 | 7.7 |
| 1910 | 2,565 | 17,596 | 60.9 | 49.0 | 4.7 |
| 11 | 3,139 | 17,762 | 62.0 | 50.0 | 3.0 |
| 12 | 3,416 | 17,841 | 63.6 | 51.0 | 3.2 |
| 13 | 4,135 | 17,920 | 65.3 | 52.0 | 2.1 |
| 14 | 4,145 | 17,998 | 63.6 | 52.0 | 3.3 |
| 15 | 4,359 | 18,077 | 79.5 | 56.0 | 1.1 |
| 16 | 4,644 | 18,155 | 91.3 | 62.0 | 0.4 |
| 17 | 5,499 | 18,234 | 113.9 | 74.0 | 0.6 |
| 18 | 6,533 | 18,312 | 130.1 | 99.0 | 0.8 |
| 19 | 7,926 | 18,391 | 140.8 | 120.0 | 2.1 |
| 1920 | 8,348 | 18,469 | 170.9 | 148.0 | 2.0 |
| 21 | 6,633 | 18,548 | 126.8 | 142.0 | 12.9 |
| 22 | 5,625 | 17,804 | 115.0 | 110.0 | 14.3 |
| 23 | 5,429 | 17,965 | 112.8 | 98.0 | 11.7 |

# TABLE E.1 (*contd.*)

| Year | Total Union Membership (000s) | Potential Union Membership (000s) | Retail Prices (1930 = 100) | Wage Earnings (1930 = 100) | Unemployment (%) |
|---|---|---|---|---|---|
| 24 | 5,544 | 18,125 | 115.0 | 102.0 | 10.3 |
| 25 | 5,506 | 18,286 | 111.8 | 103.0 | 11.3 |
| 26 | 5,219 | 18,446 | 110.7 | 102.0 | 12.5 |
| 27 | 4,919 | 18,609 | 105.3 | 103.0 | 9.7 |
| 28 | 4,806 | 18,771 | 105.3 | 101.0 | 10.8 |
| 29 | 4,858 | 18,934 | 104.3 | 101.0 | 10.4 |
| 1930 | 4,842 | 19,096 | 100.0 | 100.0 | 16.0 |
| 31 | 4,624 | 19,259 | 92.4 | 99.0 | 21.3 |
| 32 | 4,444 | 19,340 | 90.3 | 97.0 | 22.1 |
| 33 | 4,392 | 19,422 | 89.2 | 96.0 | 19.9 |
| 34 | 4,590 | 19,503 | 89.2 | 97.0 | 16.7 |
| 35 | 4,867 | 19,585 | 92.4 | 100.0 | 15.5 |
| 36 | 5,295 | 19,666 | 94.6 | 103.0 | 13.1 |
| 37 | 5,842 | 19,748 | 100.0 | 106.0 | 10.8 |
| 38 | 6,053 | 19,829 | 98.9 | 109.0 | 13.5 |
| 39 | 6,298 | 19,911 | 101.0 | n.a. | 11.6 |
| 1940 | 6,613 | 19,992 | 114.5 | 141.0 | 9.7 |
| 41 | 7,165 | 20,074 | 124.7 | 154.0 | 6.6 |
| 42 | 7,866 | 20,155 | 132.3 | 174.0 | 2.4 |
| 43 | 8,174 | 20,237 | 138.0 | 191.0 | 0.8 |
| 44 | 8,087 | 20,318 | 140.6 | 198.0 | 0.7 |
| 45 | 7,875 | 20,400 | 145.7 | 196.0 | 1.2 |
| 46 | 8,803 | 20,481 | 150.8 | 207.0 | 2.5 |
| 47 | 9,145 | 20,563 | 159.0 | 221.0 | 3.1 |
| 48 | 9,363 | 20,732 | 169.8 | 239.0 | 1.8 |
| 49 | 9,318 | 20,782 | 174.9 | 249.0 | 1.6 |
| 1950 | 9,289 | 21,055 | 180.5 | 262.9 | 1.6 |
| 51 | 9,530 | 21,177 | 197.1 | 289.5 | 1.3 |
| 52 | 9,588 | 21,252 | 215.0 | 312.3 | 2.2 |
| 53 | 9,527 | 21,352 | 221.8 | 331.6 | 1.8 |
| 54 | 9,566 | 21,658 | 225.9 | 353.2 | 1.5 |
| 55 | 9,741 | 21,913 | 236.0 | 386.0 | 1.2 |
| 56 | 9,778 | 22,180 | 247.8 | 416.9 | 1.3 |
| 57 | 9,829 | 22,334 | 257.0 | 436.2 | 1.6 |
| 58 | 9,639 | 22,290 | 264.6 | 451.2 | 2.2 |
| 59 | 9,623 | 22,429 | 266.0 | 471.7 | 2.3 |
| 1960 | 9,835 | 22,817 | 268.8 | 502.2 | 1.7 |
| 61 | 9,916 | 23,112 | 278.0 | 532.7 | 1.6 |
| 62 | 10,014 | 23,432 | 289.8 | 551.6 | 2.1 |
| 63 | 10,067 | 23,558 | 295.7 | 574.8 | 2.6 |
| 64 | 10,218 | 23,706 | 305.4 | 624.5 | 1.7 |
| 65 | 10,325 | 23,920 | 320.0 | 674.7 | 1.5 |
| 66 | 10,262 | 24,065 | 332.5 | 714.1 | 1.6 |
| 67 | 10,190 | 23,807 | 340.5 | 742.3 | 2.5 |
| 68 | 10,193 | 23,667 | 356.6 | 803.3 | 2.5 |
| 69 | 10,472 | 23,603 | 375.9 | 870.4 | 2.5 |
| 1970 | 11,179 | 23,446 | 400.0 | 988.6 | 2.6 |

## Appendix E

SOURCES AND NOTES:
*Trade Union Membership.* The trade union membership figures are those published annually by the Department of Employment. See, for example, 'Membership of Trade Unions in 1974'. *Department of Employment Gazette*, LXXXIII (November 1975), 1118–19. The 1964–70 figures are provisional and subject to revision as additional information becomes available. The latest revised figure has been used for each year. A full description of this series as well as an assessment of its strengths and weaknesses is given in G. S. Bain, R. Bacon, and J. Pimlott, 'The Labour Force', *Trends in British Society since 1900*, ed. A. H. Halsey (London: Macmillan, 1972), 109–11.

*Potential Union Membership.* The potential union membership figures for 1948–68 are from *British Labour Statistics: Historical Abstract* (London: HMSO, 1971), table 125; for 1969 and 1970, the figures are from 'Numbers of Employees (Employed and Unemployed)', *Department of Employment Gazette* (February 1970 and February 1971). The pre-1948 figures are derived from the Census of Population with linear interpolations for the intervening years. All the figures exclude exployers, the self-employed, and members of the armed forces, but include the unemployed. See Bain, Bacon, and Pimlott, *op. cit.*, 111.

*Retail Prices.* For 1892–1939, the retail price index is derived from E. H. Phelps Brown and S. V. Hopkins, 'The Course of Wage-Rates in Five Countries, 1860–1939', *Oxford Economic Papers*, New Series, II (June 1950), 276 and 281, which in turn is based on Bowley's index for 1900–14 and the Ministry of Labour's index for 1914–39. For 1940–49, the index is derived from London and Cambridge Economic Service, *The British Economy: Key Statistics, 1900–1966* (London: Times Newspapers, n.d.), which in turn is based on R. G. D. Allen's estimates for 1940–47 and the Ministry of Labour's estimates for 1947–9. For 1950–68, the index is derived from *Statistics on Incomes, Prices, Employment and Production*, no. 29 (June 1969), 8. The figures for 1969–70 were supplied by the Department of Employment from unpublished data and are comparable to those for 1950–68. A full description of this series as well as an assessment of its strengths and weaknesses is given in Bain, Bacon, and Pimlott, *op. cit.*, 107–9.

*Wage Earnings.* The wage earnings index for 1892–1949 is taken from A. L. Bowley, *Wages and Income in the United Kingdom since 1860* (Cambridge: Cambridge University Press, 1937), and *idem*, 'Index Numbers of Wage Rates and Cost of Living', *Journal of the Royal Statistical Society*, Series A, CXV (1952), 500–506; those for 1950–68 are from *Statistics on Incomes, Prices, Employment and Production, loc. cit.*; and those for 1969–70 were supplied by the Department of Employment from unpublished data and are comparable to those for 1950–68. No data are available for 1937 and 1939. A 1937 figure was obtained by taking the mid-point between the 1936 and 1938 figures. The difference between the 1938 and 1940 figures is too great, however, to allow a 1939 figure to be derived in a similar way. Hence there is no rate of change of wages figure for 1939 and 1940. A full description of the series as well as an assessment of its strengths and weaknesses is given in Bain, Bacon, and Pimlott, *op. cit.*, 105–7.

*Unemployment.* The figures for 1892–1912 are the percentage unemployed in certain trade unions and are taken from B. R. Mitchell and P. M. Deane, *Abstract of British Historical Statistics* (Cambridge: Cambridge University Press, 1962);

those for 1913–21 are the percentage unemployed in certain trade unions as adjusted by J. Hilton, 'Statistics of Unemployment Derived from the Working of the Unemployment Insurance Acts', *Journal of the Royal Statistical Society*, LXXXVI (March 1923), 154–205, and cited by LCES, *op. cit.*; those for 1922–47 are the insured unemployed as a percentage of the insured labour force as given by the Ministry of Labour and adjusted by LCES to obtain greater comparability across a period which saw several changes in the coverage of the unemployment insurance legislation; those for 1948–66 are the number registered as unemployed as a percentage of the estimated total number of employees as given by *British Labour Statistics: Historical Abstract, op. cit.*, table 165; and those for 1967–70 are on a comparable basis and are from the *British Labour Statistics Year Book 1973* (London: HMSO, 1975), table 94. A full description of the series as well as an assessment of its strengths and weaknesses is given in Bain, Bacon, and Pimlott, *op. cit.*, 102–4.

## TABLE E.2
## THE BASIC DATA FOR THE UNITED STATES

| Year | Total Union Membership (000s) | Potential Union Membership (000s) | Retail Prices (1957–59 = 100) | Wage Earnings ($) | Unemployment (%) |
|------|-------------------------------|------------------------------------|-------------------------------|-------------------|------------------|
| 1897 | 447 | 14,792 | 29.0 | 0.176 | 14.5 |
| 98 | 501 | 15,001 | 29.0 | 0.173 | 12.4 |
| 99 | 611 | 15,391 | 29.0 | 0.181 | 6.5 |
| 1900 | 869 | 15,686 | 29.0 | 0.186 | 5.0 |
| 1 | 1,125 | 16,216 | 29.0 | 0.193 | 4.0 |
| 2 | 1,376 | 16,872 | 30.0 | 0.200 | 3.7 |
| 3 | 1,914 | 17,628 | 31.0 | 0.204 | 3.9 |
| 4 | 2,073 | 18,385 | 31.0 | 0.203 | 5.4 |
| 5 | 2,022 | 19,172 | 31.0 | 0.206 | 4.3 |
| 6 | 1,907 | 19,862 | 32.0 | 0.218 | 1.7 |
| 7 | 2,080 | 20,805 | 33.0 | 0.224 | 2.8 |
| 8 | 2,131 | 21,703 | 32.0 | 0.218 | 8.0 |
| 9 | 2,006 | 22,341 | 32.0 | 0.220 | 5.1 |
| 1910 | 2,102 | 23,381 | 33.0 | 0.231 | 5.9 |
| 11 | 2,246 | 24,097 | 33.0 | 0.235 | 6.7 |
| 12 | 2,335 | 24,400 | 34.0 | 0.240 | 4.6 |
| 13 | 2,588 | 25,060 | 34.5 | 0.253 | 4.3 |
| 14 | 2,566 | 25,926 | 35.0 | 0.252 | 7.9 |
| 15 | 2,478 | 26,240 | 35.4 | 0.258 | 8.5 |
| 16 | 2,656 | 26,723 | 38.0 | 0.292 | 5.1 |
| 17 | 2,912 | 26,828 | 44.7 | 0.344 | 4.6 |
| 18 | 3,285 | 26,053 | 52.4 | 0.440 | 1.4 |
| 19 | 3,849 | 26,824 | 60.3 | 0.472 | 1.4 |
| 1920 | 4,775 | 28,658 | 69.8 | 0.549 | 5.2 |
| 21 | 4,553 | 29,369 | 62.3 | 0.509 | 11.7 |
| 22 | 3,821 | 29,492 | 58.4 | 0.482 | 6.7 |
| 23 | 3,418 | 30,247 | 59.4 | 0.516 | 2.4 |
| 24 | 3,334 | 31,118 | 59.6 | 0.541 | 5.0 |
| 25 | 3,319 | 31,825 | 61.1 | 0.541 | 3.2 |

## TABLE E.2 (*contd.*)

| Year | Total Union Membership (000s) | Potential Union Membership (000s) | Retail Prices (1957–59 = 100) | Wage Earnings ($) | Unemployment (%) |
|------|------|------|------|------|------|
| 26 | 3,299 | 32,296 | 61.6 | 0.542 | 1.8 |
| 27 | 3,343 | 33,131 | 60.5 | 0.544 | 3.3 |
| 28 | 3,269 | 33,890 | 59.7 | 0.556 | 4.2 |
| 29 | 3,213 | 34,649 | 59.7 | 0.560 | 3.2 |
| 1930 | 3,162 | 35,515 | 58.2 | 0.546 | 8.9 |
| 31 | 3,142 | 36,418 | 53.0 | 0.509 | 16.3 |
| 32 | 2,968 | 37,360 | 47.6 | 0.441 | 24.1 |
| 33 | 2,805 | 38,164 | 45.1 | 0.437 | 25.2 |
| 34 | 3,448 | 38,944 | 46.6 | 0.526 | 22.0 |
| 35 | 3,609 | 39,479 | 47.8 | 0.544 | 20.3 |
| 36 | 3,932 | 40,116 | 48.3 | 0.550 | 17.0 |
| 37 | 5,563 | 40,861 | 50.0 | 0.617 | 14.3 |
| 38 | 5,850 | 41,792 | 49.1 | 0.620 | 19.1 |
| 39 | 6,339 | 42,410 | 48.4 | 0.627 | 17.2 |
| 1940 | 7,055 | 42,890 | 48.8 | 0.655 | 14.6 |
| 41 | 8,410 | 43,040 | 51.3 | 0.726 | 9.9 |
| 42 | 9,818 | 44,090 | 56.8 | 0.851 | 4.7 |
| 43 | 11,383 | 43,560 | 60.3 | 0.957 | 1.9 |
| 44 | 12,153 | 42,560 | 61.3 | 1.011 | 1.2 |
| 45 | 12,088 | 41,790 | 62.7 | 1.016 | 1.9 |
| 46 | 12,684 | 44,850 | 68.0 | 1.075 | 3.9 |
| 47 | 13,968 | 47,107 | 77.8 | 1.217 | 3.9 |
| 48 | 14,339 | 48,145 | 83.8 | 1.328 | 3.8 |
| 49 | 13,977 | 48,809 | 83.0 | 1.378 | 5.9 |
| 1950 | 14,090 | 50,277 | 83.8 | 1.440 | 5.3 |
| 51 | 14,968 | 50,652 | 90.5 | 1.560 | 3.3 |
| 52 | 15,452 | 51,046 | 92.5 | 1.650 | 3.1 |
| 53 | 16,404 | 51,983 | 93.2 | 1.740 | 2.9 |
| 54 | 15,679 | 52,514 | 93.6 | 1.780 | 5.6 |
| 55 | 16,043 | 53,848 | 93.3 | 1.860 | 4.4 |
| 56 | 16,396 | 55,393 | 94.7 | 1.950 | 4.2 |
| 57 | 16,624 | 55,950 | 98.0 | 2.050 | 4.3 |
| 58 | 15,650 | 56,927 | 100.7 | 2.110 | 6.8 |
| 59 | 15,449 | 57,585 | 101.5 | 2.190 | 5.5 |
| 1960 | 15,539 | 59,031 | 103.1 | 2.260 | 5.6 |
| 61 | 15,798 | 59,942 | 104.2 | 2.320 | 6.7 |
| 62 | 15,937 | 60,436 | 105.4 | 2.390 | 5.5 |
| 63 | 16,194 | 62,023 | 106.7 | 2.460 | 5.7 |
| 64 | 16,551 | 63,281 | 108.1 | 2.530 | 5.2 |
| 65 | 16,977 | 64,783 | 109.9 | 2.610 | 4.5 |
| 66 | 17,539 | 66,502 | 113.1 | 2.720 | 3.8 |
| 67 | 17,191 | 69,124 | 116.3 | 2.830 | 3.8 |
| 68 | 17,703 | 70,615 | 121.2 | 3.010 | 3.6 |
| 69 | 17,815 | 72,536 | 127.7 | 3.190 | 3.5 |
| 70 | 18,136 | 74,687 | 135.3 | 3.360 | 4.9 |

SOURCES AND NOTES:

*Trade Union Membership.* There are basically two union membership series for the United States: one is compiled by the National Bureau of Economic Research and the other by the Bureau of Labor Statistics. The series used in this study is based on that produced by the NBER. Since this series stops in 1966, the figures for 1967–70 were obtained as predicted values from the linear regression of the NBER series on the BLS series for the overlapping period. For a full description of this series as well as an assessment of its strength and weaknesses, see G. S. Bain and R. J. Price, *Profiles of Union Growth* (Oxford: Blackwell, forthcoming).

*Potential Union Membership.* For 1948–70, the potential union membership series is from *Manpower Report of the President* (Washington: USGPO, 1973), tables A-1 and A-13. The series was derived by subtracting from the civilian labour force the total number of self-employed and family workers. Alternatively, the series can be derived by adding together the unemployed and the total number of wage and salary workers. In short, the series excludes employers, the self-employed, and unpaid family workers, but includes the unemployed. For 1900–47, the potential union membership series is from Stanley Lebergott, *Manpower in Economic Growth: The American Record since 1800* (New York: McGraw-Hill, 1964), tables A-3 and A-4. The figures were derived by adding together the unemployed, domestic service employees, and farm and non-farm employees. For 1897–9, the figures were derived from the civilian labour force figure given in *ibid.*, table A-15. Since there are no data for these years on the number of employers, self-employed, and unpaid family workers, it was assumed that union potential made up the same proportion of the civilian labour force in 1897–9 as it did in 1900 (55.3 per cent).

*Retail Prices.* For 1897–1968, the retail price series is from the *Handbook of Labor Statistics 1969* (Washington: US Department of Labor, Bureau of Labor Statistics, 1969), table 108. For 1969–70, the data are from the *Monthly Labor Review* (January 1971), 102, table 25; (August 1971), 106, table 25.

*Wage Earnings.* For 1969–70, the wage earnings series is from *Monthly Labor Review*, XCIV (August 1971), 103, table 21. The figures represent the average hourly earnings of production workers in manufacturing industries. For 1919–68, the figures are on a comparable basis and are from the *Handbook of Labor Statistics 1969, op. cit.*, table 84. Before 1919, the official series is incomplete. But Rees has compiled a similar but distinct average hourly earnings series for manufacturing which covers the period 1890–1957. See Albert Rees, *Real Wages in Manufacturing, 1890–1914* (New York: Princeton University Press for the National Bureau of Economic Research, 1960), table 1; and *idem, New Measures of Wage Earner Compensation in Manufacturing, 1914–57* (New York: National Bureau of Economic Research, 1960), table 1. Hence data for 1897–1918 were obtained as predicted values from the linear regression of the official series on the Rees series for the overlapping period.

*Unemployment.* For 1897–9, the figures are from Lebergott, *op. cit.*, table A-15. For 1900–60, they are from *ibid.*, table A-3. For 1961–70, they are from the *Manpower Report of the President, op. cit.*, table A-1.

## Appendix E

### TABLE E.3
### THE BASIC DATA FOR AUSTRALIA

| Year | Total Union Membership (000s) | Potential Union Membership (000s) | Retail Prices (1911 = 100) | Wage Rates (1911 = 100) | Unemployment (%) |
|---|---|---|---|---|---|
| 1907 | 194.6 | 1,302.9 | 90 | 89.3 | 3.6 |
| 8 | 240.5 | 1,347.6 | 95 | 90.0 | 3.9 |
| 9 | 273.5 | 1,392.3 | 95 | 92.3 | 3.7 |
| 1910 | 302.1 | 1,437.0 | 97 | 95.5 | 3.6 |
| 11 | 364.7 | 1,481.7 | 100 | 100.0 | 2.9 |
| 12 | 433.2 | 1,549.8 | 110 | 105.1 | 2.9 |
| 13 | 497.9 | 1,596.7 | 110 | 107.6 | 3.3 |
| 14 | 523.3 | 1,594.3 | 114 | 108.1 | 4.6 |
| 15 | 528.0 | 1,587.9 | 130 | 109.2 | 3.8 |
| 16 | 546.6 | 1,507.6 | 132 | 114.4 | 3.7 |
| 17 | 564.2 | 1,457.0 | 141 | 122.6 | 3.7 |
| 18 | 581.8 | 1,465.3 | 150 | 127.0 | 3.8 |
| 19 | 627.7 | 1,512.3 | 170 | 137.0 | 3.6 |
| 1920 | 684.5 | 1,623.2 | 193 | 162.7 | 4.6 |
| 21 | 703.0 | 1,711.4 | 168 | 182.6 | 5.9 |
| 22 | 702.9 | 1,742.6 | 162 | 180.1 | 5.0 |
| 23 | 699.7 | 1,782.2 | 166 | 180.5 | 4.9 |
| 24 | 729.2 | 1,842.0 | 164 | 184.0 | 5.5 |
| 25 | 795.7 | 1,888.9 | 165 | 186.1 | 5.6 |
| 26 | 851.5 | 1,910.4 | 168 | 191.4 | 4.6 |
| 27 | 911.7 | 1,949.1 | 166 | 194.6 | 5.2 |
| 28 | 911.5 | 1,971.9 | 167 | 196.3 | 6.5 |
| 29 | 901.2 | 1,971.6 | 171 | 197.2 | 8.2 |
| 1930 | 855.8 | 1,968.8 | 162 | 193.9 | 13.6 |
| 31 | 769.0 | 1,989.3 | 145 | 175.2 | 17.9 |
| 32 | 740.8 | 2,057.7 | 138 | 163.9 | 19.1 |
| 33 | 739.4 | 2,119.6 | 133 | 158.4 | 17.4 |
| 34 | 762.6 | 2,159.3 | 136 | 159.0 | 15.0 |
| 35 | 790.8 | 2,188.8 | 138 | 161.2 | 12.5 |
| 36 | 814.8 | 2,196.8 | 141 | 163.8 | 9.9 |
| 37 | 856.3 | 2,224.8 | 145 | 170.7 | 8.1 |
| 38 | 885.2 | 2,280.5 | 149 | 179.9 | 8.1 |
| 39 | 915.5 | 2,333.1 | 153 | 184.6 | 8.9 |
| 1940 | 955.9 | 2,365.0 | 159 | 188.9 | 6.9 |
| 41 | 1,075.7 | 2,424.8 | 167 | 199.7 | 3.4 |
| 42 | 1,182.4 | 2,534.5 | 181 | 216.4 | 1.4 |
| 43 | 1,204.9 | 2,618.8 | 188 | 230.9 | 1.0 |
| 44 | 1,218.8 | 2,643.4 | 187 | 232.6 | 1.1 |
| 45 | 1,200.4 | 2,609.3 | 187 | 233.9 | 1.7 |
| 46 | 1,284.4 | 2,558.9 | 190 | 240.0 | 2.5 |
| 47 | 1,365.5 | 2,580.2 | 198 | 259.8 | 2.4 |
| 48 | 1,455.8 | 2,669.2 | 218 | 291.4 | 1.9 |
| 49 | 1,520.9 | 2,758.2 | 240 | 321.0 | 1.6 |
| 1950 | 1,605.3 | 2,867.1 | 262 | 359.6 | 1.4 |
| 51 | 1,690.3 | 2,963.6 | 313 | 449.5 | 1.3 |

140

TABLE E.3 (*contd.*)

| Year | Total Union Membership (000s) | Potential Union Membership (000s) | Retail Prices (1911 = 100) | Wage Rates (1911 = 100) | Unemployment (%) |
|---|---|---|---|---|---|
| 52 | 1,637.5 | 2,958.9 | 367 | 524.1 | 2.2 |
| 53 | 1,679.8 | 2,947.3 | 383 | 553.9 | 2.5 |
| 54 | 1,787.5 | 3,028.8 | 386 | 563.2 | 1.7 |
| 55 | 1,801.9 | 3,121.7 | 394 | 577.3 | 1.4 |
| 56 | 1,811.4 | 3,208.5 | 419 | 604.6 | 1.8 |
| 57 | 1,810.2 | 3,266.8 | 429 | 613.5 | 2.3 |
| 58 | 1,811.2 | 3,327.4 | 435 | 624.1 | 2.7 |
| 59 | 1,850.7 | 3,379.8 | 443 | 667.0 | 2.6 |
| 1960 | 1,912.4 | 3,506.5 | 459 | 687.6 | 2.5 |
| 61 | 1,894.6 | 3,537.5 | 471 | 708.8 | 2.5 |
| 62 | 1,950.5 | 3,599.4 | 469 | 710.5 | 1.9 |
| 63 | 2,003.5 | 3,689.9 | 472 | 728.3 | 1.6 |
| 64 | 2,054.8 | 3,802.9 | 483 | 769.6 | 1.2 |
| 65 | 2,116.2 | 3,944.9 | 502 | 791.3 | 1.2 |
| 66 | 2,123.5 | 4,064.6 | 517 | 836.4 | 1.5 |
| 67 | 2,151.3 | 4,178.5 | 534 | 874.9 | 1.6 |
| 68 | 2,190.7 | 4,304.8 | 548 | 953.5 | 1.5 |
| 69 | 2,239.1 | 4,443.3 | 564 | 1,010.4 | 1.6 |

NOTES AND SOURCES:

*Trade Union Membership.* The union membership data are those compiled by the Commonwealth Bureau of Census and Statistics. A full description of the series as well as an assessment of its strengths and weaknesses is given in G. S. Bain and R. J. Price, *Profiles of Union Growth* (Oxford: Blackwell, forthcoming).

*Potential Union Membership.* For 1907–46, the potential union membership series is derived from data provided by M. Keating, 'Australian Work Force and Employment, 1910–11 to 1960–67', *Australian Economic History Review*, VII (September 1967), 150–71; and N. G. Butlin and J. A. Dowie, 'Estimates of Australian Work Force and Employment, 1861–1961', *Australian Economic History Review*, IX (September 1969), 138–55. The data for 1907–10 are derived from a linear interpolation between the 1901 and 1911 estimates. For 1947–69, the series is derived from *Labour Report*, no. 55 (Canberra: Commonwealth Bureau of Census and Statistics, 1970), 242. A full description of the series as well as an assessment of its strengths and weaknesses is given in Bain and Price, *op. cit.*

*Retail Prices.* The retail price series is from *Labour Report*, no. 56 (Canberra: Commonwealth Bureau of Census and Statistics, 1971), 41. The series is derived by linking a number of indexes that differ greatly in scope: from 1907 to 1914, the 'A' Series Retail Price Index; from 1914 to 1946–7, the 'C' Series Retail Price Index; from 1946–7 to 1948–9, a composite of the Consumer Price Index Housing Group (partly estimated) and 'C' Series Index excluding rent; and from 1948–9 to 1969 the Consumer Price Index.

## Appendix E

*Wage Rates.* For 1907–9, the wage rate data are from *Labour and Industrial Branch Report*, no. 5 (Melbourne: Commonwealth Bureau of Census and Statistics, 1914), 51–3; for 1910–46, they are from *Labour Report*, no. 36 (Canberra: Commonwealth Bureau of Census and Statistics, 1947), 71; and for 1947–55, they are from *Labour Report*, no. 44 (Canberra: Commonwealth Bureau of Census and Statistics, 1955–6), 201. The figures relate to the annual average weekly rates of pay for adult manual males in Australia. The series was discontinued in the mid 1950s. A similar series for 1939–69 is given in *Labour Report, no. 71, op. cit.,* 348. The main difference between the two series is that the former includes agriculture while the latter does not. Hence data for 1956–69 were obtained as predicted values from the linear regression of the 1907–55 series on the 1939–69 series for the overlapping period.

*Unemployment.* The unemployment series is that used by Sharpe. It is based on data from Keating, *op. cit.,* for 1912–61 and from the Commonwealth Statistician's Office for 1962–9. For 1907–11, the series is estimated from data relating to unemployment amongst trade unionists. See Ian G. Sharpe, 'The Growth of Australian Trade Unions: 1907–1969', *Journal of Industrial Relations,* XIII (June 1971), 145 and 151–2.

## TABLE E.4
## THE BASIC DATA FOR SWEDEN

| Year | Total Union Membership (000s) | Potential Union Membership (000s) | Retail Prices (1914 = 100) | Wage Earnings (öre) | Unemployment (%) |
|------|------|------|------|------|------|
| 1914 | 159.1 | 1,600.2 | 100 | 39 | 7.3 |
| 15 | 173.8 | 1,633.9 | 115 | 41 | 7.2 |
| 16 | 215.6 | 1,670.5 | 130 | 43 | 4.0 |
| 17 | 288.4 | 1,676.4 | 164 | 55 | 4.0 |
| 18 | 350.2 | 1,702.3 | 232 | 80 | 4.6 |
| 19 | 424.1 | 1,736.7 | 268 | 107 | 5.5 |
| 1920 | 469.8 | 1,784.8 | 269 | 140 | 5.4 |
| 21 | 427.6 | 1,645.6 | 231 | 138 | 26.6 |
| 22 | 413.3 | 1,663.4 | 187 | 100 | 22.9 |
| 23 | 436.6 | 1,714.9 | 174 | 95 | 12.5 |
| 24 | 495.0 | 1,722.2 | 174 | 97 | 10.1 |
| 25 | 522.6 | 1,733.8 | 177 | 100 | 11.0 |
| 26 | 551.9 | 1,777.7 | 171 | 100 | 12.2 |
| 27 | 572.2 | 1,799.1 | 169 | 102 | 12.0 |
| 28 | 605.1 | 1,843.7 | 170 | 104 | 10.6 |
| 29 | 647.1 | 1,885.7 | 168 | 106 | 10.2 |
| 1930 | 698.2 | 2,132.8 | 163 | 109 | 11.9 |
| 31 | 738.0 | 2,074.0 | 158 | 109 | 16.8 |
| 32 | 752.1 | 2,002.6 | 155 | 107 | 22.4 |
| 33 | 753.1 | 1,968.1 | 151 | 104 | 23.3 |
| 34 | 774.7 | 2,042.3 | 152 | 104 | 18.0 |
| 35 | 821.8 | 2,108.2 | 155 | 106 | 15.0 |
| 36 | 898.3 | 2,162.2 | 157 | 106 | 12.7 |
| 37 | 990.8 | 2,193.5 | 161 | 108 | 10.8 |

TABLE E.4 (*contd.*)

| Year | Total Union Membership (000s) | Potential Union Membership (000s) | Retail Prices (1914 = 100) | Wage Earnings (öre) | Unemployment (%) |
|---|---|---|---|---|---|
| 38 | 1,055.6 | 2,232.2 | 165 | 116 | 10.9 |
| 39 | 1,118.0 | 2,313.9 | 169 | 118 | 9.2 |
| 1940 | 1,136.5 | 2,188.7 | 190 | 128 | 11.8 |
| 41 | 1,157.7 | 2,184.9 | 215 | 139 | 11.3 |
| 42 | 1,210.2 | 2,261.8 | 232 | 152 | 7.5 |
| 43 | 1,246.8 | 2,313.7 | 235 | 159 | 5.7 |
| 44 | 1,296.9 | 2,321.5 | 234 | 164 | 4.9 |
| 45 | 1,356.7 | 2,366.9 | 233 | 173 | 4.5 |
| 46 | 1,413.6 | 2,403.7 | 234 | 187 | 3.2 |
| 47 | 1,486.8 | 2,454.9 | 240 | 215 | 2.8 |
| 48 | 1,548.5 | 2,459.5 | 252 | 234 | 2.8 |
| 49 | 1,575.5 | 2,455.9 | 256 | 243 | 2.7 |
| 1950 | 1,614.0 | 2,456.0 | 259 | 253 | 2.2 |
| 51 | 1,680.5 | 2,488.7 | 300 | 305 | 1.8 |
| 52 | 1,725.6 | 2,521.4 | 324 | 363 | 2.4 |
| 53 | 1,736.9 | 2,554.1 | 328 | 379 | 2.8 |
| 54 | 1,751.9 | 2,586.8 | 330 | 394 | 2.6 |
| 55 | 1,799.0 | 2,619.5 | 339 | 426 | 2.5 |
| 56 | 1,827.4 | 2,652.2 | 356 | 462 | 1.5 |
| 57 | 1,856.6 | 2,684.9 | 372 | 490 | 1.9 |
| 58 | 1,897.3 | 2,717.6 | 388 | 521 | 2.5 |
| 59 | 1,930.8 | 2,750.3 | 391 | 544 | 2.0 |
| 1960 | 1,973.4 | 2,783.0 | 407 | 577 | 1.4 |
| 61 | 2,018.5 | 2,827.0 | 416 | 623 | 1.2 |
| 62 | 2,072.3 | 2,871.0 | 436 | 678 | 1.3 |
| 63 | 2,120.7 | 2,915.0 | 449 | 729 | 1.4 |
| 64 | 2,164.9 | 2,959.0 | 463 | 794 | 1.1 |
| 65 | 2,198.3 | 3,003.0 | 486 | 878 | 1.1 |
| 66 | 2,261.4 | 3,024.9 | 518 | 960 | 1.4 |
| 67 | 2,310.6 | 2,988.0 | 540 | 1,044 | 1.7 |
| 68 | 2,363.4 | 3,025.4 | 550 | 1,117 | 2.0 |
| 69 | 2,430.3 | 3,057.2 | 566 | 1,215 | 1.7 |
| 1970 | 2,499.6 | 3,083.5 | 605 | 1,352 | 1.5 |

NOTES AND SOURCES:
*Trade Union Membership.* The trade union membership series is from G. S. Bain and R. J. Price, *Profiles of Union Growth* (Oxford: Blackwell, forthcoming). This work gives a full description of the series as well as an assessment of its strengths and weaknesses.

*Potential Union Membership.* For 1914–50, the data are from Karl G. Jungenfelt, *Löneandelen och den ekonomiska utvecklingen* (Stockholm: Almqvist and Wiksell, 1966), table 1. For 1951–70, they are from the Census of Population with linear interpolations for the inter-Censal years.

*Retail Prices.* The index is from *Statistiska Meddelanden* (Stockholm: National Central Bureau of Statistics, Pa. 1971:4), 17, table 4. It is described as a cost-of-living index excluding direct taxes.

*Wage Earnings.* The data for 1939—70 are from *Loner 1970*, II (Stockholm: National Central Bureau of Statistics, 1972), 75, table 10. They represent the hourly earnings of male and female manual workers in manufacturing and mining. The series does not exist prior to 1939. For the period 1913—51, *Lönestatistisk Årsbok För Sverige* (1934), 52, table 13; (1951), 72, table 35 gives a series with a slightly wider industrial coverage but with rates of change similar to the above series for the overlapping period. Hence data for 1914—38 were obtained as predicted values from a linear regression of the 1939—70 series on the 1913—51 series for the overlapping period.

*Unemployment.* For 1969—70, the data are from *Statistisk Årsbok För Sverige* (Stockholm: National Central Bureau of Statistics, 1973), table 248. For 1956—68, the data are from *Statistisk Årsbok För Sverige* (Stockholm: National Central Bureau of Statistics, 1969), table 235. The figures represent the annual average number of insured unemployed as a percentage of those who are members of the unemployment insurance scheme. For 1914—55, the figures were supplied by Bo Jonsson of the LO and represent the extent of unemployment among trade union members. These data are also given in *Historisk Statistik För Sverige*, III (Stockholm: National Central Bureau of Statistics, 1960), table 121, for the period 1931—50.

# Index

154